EAT WELL ~ BE WELL Cookbook ~

By Metropolitan Life Insurance Company
Health and Safety Education Division
New York

A Fireside Book
Published by Simon & Schuster, Inc.
New York

A Fireside Book
Published by Simon & Schuster, Inc.
Simon & Schuster Building
Rockefeller Center
1230 Avenue of the Americas
New York, New York 10020

FIRESIDE and colophon are registered trademarks of
Simon & Schuster, Inc.

Manufactured in the United States of America

10 9 8 7 6 5 4 3 2 1

Library of Congress Cataloging-in-Publication Data

Eat Well, Be Well® Cookbook.

   "A Fireside book."
   Bibliography: p.
   Includes index.
   1. Low-calories diet—Recipes. 2. Low-fat diet—
Recipes. I. Becker, Gail L. II. Hammock, Delia A.
III. Metropolitan Life Insurance Company.
RM222.2.E237 1986   641.5'635   86-13100
ISBN 0-671-62895-X

EAT WELL, BE WELL® Cookbook

Writers: Gail L. Becker, R.D.
Delia A. Hammock, M.S., R.D.

Editors: Laura W. Conway, M.S., R.D.
Marsha Hudnall, M.S., R.D.

Recipe Development: Catherine Paukner

Art and Design: Evelyne Johnson Associates Inc.

Illustrations: Ted Enik

Cover Design: Barry Littmann

Consultants:

Victor Herbert, M.D., J.D.
Professor of Medicine
and Chairman
Committee to Strengthen
Nutrition
Mount Sinai Medical
Center, NY
and
Bronx VA Medical Center, NY

Artemis P. Simopoulos, M.D.
Chairman, Nutrition Coordinating
Committee
National Institutes of Health
Department of Health and Human
Services
Bethesda, Md.

Metropolitan Life Insurance Company

Health and Safety Education Division

Clarence E. Pearson, Assistant Vice-President
Doris Bressler, Director of Health Communications
Carole A. Passadin, Health Education Consultant

The *Eat Well, Be Well*® Cookbook contains reliable and up-to-date information. However, individuals should consult a physician before attempting to gain or lose weight or treat ailments through diet.

Contents

Preface

Metropolitan Life's *Eat Well, Be Well®* Cookbook is an extension of two *Eat Well, Be Well®* television series funded by Metropolitan and shown on PBS-TV stations throughout the United States. The Dietary Guidelines for Americans, published by the U.S. Department of Agriculture and the U.S. Department of Health and Human Services, provide the basis for *Eat Well, Be Well®*. The TV series, like the cookbook, are meant to help Americans learn how to make the guidelines part of their daily lives.

The 40-segment TV series, featuring home economist and chef Helen Hatton, was produced by Amram Nowak Associates. Noted nutrition scientist Victor Herbert, M.D., was a consultant on the series and also made an invaluable contribution to this cookbook.

A third *Eat Well, Be Well®* series, prepared especially for the Instructional Television Service of PBS and addressed to children in grades one through four, premieres on public TV in the fall of 1986.

For more than 75 years, Met Life has been promoting the importance of disease prevention and health promotion through publications, films, radio and TV. The principles of good nutrition and the importance of healthful eating patterns have always received major emphasis in these mass media campaigns.

This book, with its basic nutrition information, fitness and weight control guidance, tempting recipes and useful food tips, can help you establish a lifelong pattern of eating a moderate, balanced and varied diet—the kind that more and more health experts agree promotes good health. Share this guide with your family and friends so that they, too, may Eat Well and Be Well.

Acknowledgments

Met Life is grateful to the following people:

Literary agents Dr. Stanley M. Ulanoff and Roger S. Ulanoff of ADVISIONS for their initiative and guidance.

Dr. Ash Hayes and the President's Council on Physical Fitness and Sports for their editorial consultation.

Simon and Schuster, especially editor Nancy Kalish, for orchestrating the publication and promotion of this book.

The Met Life Health and Safety Education Division staff, especially Dolores M. Keenan, Alice E. Conway, Basmatie Mohabir, Gladys Thomas, Lillian Brown, Ada J. Grippi, and Ada L. Arieta for countless production services. Also Neill Corbett and Kim Dillon, Met Life Editorial Services, for their advice.

Special Acknowledgment

Met Life gratefully acknowledges the pivotal contribution to the *Eat Well, Be Well*® project made by Artemis P. Simopoulos, M.D., Chairman of the Nutrition Coordinating Committee of the National Institutes of Health. Her concern for the nutrition education of the public and her invaluable guidance inspired the *Eat Well, Be Well*® TV series and, subsequently, this cookbook.

She is unswerving in her dedication to disseminating the most current scientific information from leading authorities to all Americans. Her generous contribution to the *Eat Well, Be Well*® project is unique in the breadth of its perspective and the depth of its commitment.

Introduction

The Eat Well, Be Well® Cookbook is Met Life's latest contribution to promoting healthy living. The Company published its first cookbook in 1918 and has issued many other versions since then.

The presence of a nutrition component in both the cause and treatment of many diseases—most notably, cardiovascular disease—as well as advances in nutrition science make nutrition education of the public a "must" today more than ever.

From the basics of nutrition and weight control, to advice and tips on changing bad eating habits, to more than 100 appealing recipes, this book can help you reach your nutrition goals. Unlike fad diets, which are at best short-term and can even be dangerous, there is no gimmick here. The recipes have been designed to help prevent some of the health problems associated with our way of life, such as obesity and high levels of cholesterol in the blood which increase the risk of heart attacks and other ailments.

This book will help you design a nutritional program that you can stick to. And, as the recipe section will prove, eating right doesn't have to be dull. Above all, eating should be fun. Mealtime is a time of sharing with family and friends. And by using the recipes in this book in a balanced weekly menu plan, you can incorporate the advances of nutrition science into your family meal patterns.

Today, Americans are healthier than ever. Life expectancy for males born in 1983 is 71 years, up from 67 years in 1969–1971 and 48 years in 1900–1902. For females born in 1983 the life expectancy is 78 years, up from 75 years in 1969–1971 and 51 years in 1900–1902. These added years are the result, in part, of the control through immunization of many of the infectious diseases of childhood. Improvements in sanitation, housing, drinking water and nutrition also have contributed years to our lives. In addition, our ability to diagnose and treat such diseases as hypertension, heart disease and diabetes have made a substantial difference.

Met Life, through its Health and Safety Education Division, has conducted campaigns for many years to raise public awareness of the major health problems of the day and what to do about them. We also have supported and participated in research and demonstration projects in cooperation with national health organizations and government health agencies. Today's heightened interest in wellness and physical fitness encourages us to reaffirm our commitment to public health education.

While interest in food and nutrition may be at its peak, many people still are confused about what to eat for good health. Unfortunately, misinformation is widely-promoted. Readers of Met Life's *Eat Well, Be Well®* *Cookbook* will find that it emphasizes *sound* nutrition principles and provides recipes for a lifetime of good eating.

Paul S. Entmacher, M.D.
Senior Vice-President
and Chief Medical Director
Metropolitan Life Insurance Company

I
First, the Basics

M. MACGOWAN

You don't have to know a lot about the science of nutrition to eat properly, but you will find it easier to plan an adequate, well-balanced diet if you understand some basic principles. Knowing about nutrition *facts* (rather than fears, media hype and myths) will also help you make informed decisions about food choices for your own needs and priorities.

What Is an Adequate Diet?

An adequate diet contains all the food components your body needs for optimum health. These components are called nutrients. And these 50 or so nutrients can be generally divided into six categories: proteins, fats, carbohydrates (these three contain calories for energy), vitamins, minerals and water. In addition, an adequate diet includes fiber for roughage.

The Seven Components of Food

Proteins

Protein is not the miracle nutrient it is often claimed to be, but it is an indispensable part of the diet. All protein is made up of smaller units called amino acids. After we eat, food proteins are broken down in the stomach and intestines into amino acids. These amino acids are then absorbed and carried by the blood to the cells throughout the body where they provide the building blocks that make all the body's own protein, including enzymes and antibodies. Protein is an important part of every living cell and is essential for the growth and maintenance of body tissue.

The human body needs 22 different kinds of amino acids. Some of these can be manufactured inside body cells, but eight amino acids (nine for infants) must be supplied by the food we eat. These are called "essential" amino acids because it is essential that they be eaten. Protein foods that contain all the essential amino acids in the proportions needed by the body are considered to be high quality or "complete" proteins. Complete proteins come from animal sources such as meat, poultry, fish, eggs, cheese and milk.

Lower quality proteins are found in breads, grains, cereals, nuts and legumes. These plant proteins are considered to be "incomplete" because they lack one or more of the essential amino acids. Combining a plant protein with a small amount of animal protein will greatly improve its quality. Macaroni and cheese, and spaghetti with meat sauce are two such combinations.

Strict vegetarians get their complete protein by the right combination of two plant proteins. When eaten together each "complements" the other by making up for the other's amino acid deficiencies. Together they create complete proteins. For example, grains with legumes, such as rice and beans, provide "complementary" protein.

The body can't store protein or amino acids. Extra protein is therefore used as energy (supplying four calories per gram), or converted to fat and stored. Protein is plentiful in the American diet, so there is no reason for a healthy person to take protein supplements of any kind.

Fats

Fats (technically known as lipids) are our most concentrated source of energy. At nine calories per gram they contain more than twice as much energy value as carbohydrates or protein. Foods high in fat often seem the most satisfying because fat is packed with calories, and because it slows down digestion so the stomach stays full longer. Fat also carries many of the components that give foods their aroma and flavor.

Most foods are a combination of nutrients, and therefore many foods contain fat. The fat in food can be visible or hidden. Visible fats include butter, margarine and oils, as well as the fat you can trim from meat. Hidden fats are an integral part of foods, and include the fat in nuts, seeds, eggs and baked goods, the butterfat in whole milk and cheese, the fat added to many foods in processing and fat marbling in meat.

There are two different types of fats—saturated and unsaturated. Most saturated fats come from animal sources and are solid at room temperature. These include butter, shortening and lard. Unsaturated fats come from vegetable sources and are liquid at room temperature. Coconut and palm oils are exceptions because, despite being liquid, they are high in saturated fats.

Unsaturated fats may be polyunsaturated, such as corn and safflower oils, or monounsaturated such as olive and peanut oils. Vegetable oils that are unsaturated in their natural state may be commercially saturated through a process called hydrogenation. Hydrogenating or partially hydrogenating oils in margarines and vegetable shortenings make them solid at room temperature and give them a longer shelf life.

Cholesterol is a necessary component of the membrane of every cell. Cholesterol is a sterol, but is usually described under lipids because saturated fats raise the cholesterol level in the blood. The body also uses cholesterol to make the sex hormones and to syn-

7

thesize vitamin D. Cholesterol in the body comes from two sources: about 15 percent comes from animal foods in the diet (including eggs and dairy products) and about 85 percent is made in the liver and in other body cells. Cholesterol is not found in any plant foods.

Carbohydrates

Carbohydrates, both simple (sugars) and complex (starches), are a major source of the body's energy and usually provide about half of the day's energy requirement. Simple sugars are found naturally as part of fruits, vegetables and milk, or as a refined product in foods such as table sugar, syrups, soda, cakes and candy. Other foods that we think of as being "starchy" contain a high proportion of complex carbohydrates. Some foods containing complex carbohydrates are bread, pasta, potatoes and cereals.

Through digestion, the body breaks down both simple and complex carbohydrates to the simple sugar glucose. Glucose supplies the energy specifically needed for the operation of the brain and nervous system, as well as the fuel for physical activity and basic body function. Extra glucose is carried to the liver, where it is converted to the complex carbohydrate glycogen for short-term storage. When the body stores of glycogen are filled, extra energy from all types of carbohydrates (as well as extra energy from protein and dietary fat) are stored as body fat.

Although carbohydrates have a long-standing reputation of being "fattening," all sugars and starches actually contain four calories per gram—the same as protein and less than half the calories of an equal amount of fat.

Vitamins

Vitamins, in very small amounts, help regulate the chemical reactions the body uses to convert food into energy and living tissue. Vitamins themselves do not supply energy. A vitamin missing from an otherwise complete diet will result in a specific deficiency disease. Scurvy results from lack of vitamin C, for example. But because of an abundant food supply and the enrichment and fortification of certain foods, deficiency diseases are rare today in the United States.

There are 13 known vitamins required to maintain human life. Vitamins A, D, E and K are fat-soluble. Vitamins C and the B-complex vitamins, including thiamin (B1), riboflavin (B2), niacin (B3), pantothenic acid, folic acid, B6, B12 and biotin, are water-soluble.

8

The fat-soluble vitamins are stored in the liver and body fat in almost unlimited amounts. If regularly taken in large quantities as a supplement, fat-soluble vitamins, particularly A and D, are toxic. Water-soluble vitamins are only stored in small amounts and therefore must be supplied regularly through the diet. Typically, most of the excesses of water-soluble vitamins are excreted in the urine. However, most B vitamins, including B6, and vitamin C, are toxic in large doses.

There are no health benefits associated with vitamin dosage in excess of the Recommended Daily Allowances (RDA) for healthy people. And, when vitamins are taken in large doses (megadoses), they are no longer nutrients and must be regarded as drugs, with the potential for toxicity and complications that any drug presents when taken into the body in large amounts for prolonged periods.

Minerals

Minerals are inorganic substances that are widely distributed in nature and are vital to many functions of the human body. The essential minerals are divided into two groups, macrominerals and trace minerals. Macrominerals—including calcium, phosphorus, magnesium, sodium, potassium, chloride and sulfur—are found in relatively large amounts in the body and are required in the diet in amounts ranging up to one gram. Trace minerals—including iron, manganese, copper, iodine, zinc, fluoride, selenium, chromium and molybdenum—are needed in far smaller amounts. Although both macrominerals and trace minerals are essential to good health, they can be harmful—even deadly—in excess. Too much of one mineral can interfere with the function of another, throwing off the body's delicate balance.

Most minerals are poisons in large quantities.

Vitamins and minerals in the proper amounts essential for good health are readily available in a balanced diet. Only a competent physician can diagnose whether you have a vitamin or mineral deficiency which requires the use of supplements. Self-dosing with vitamin and mineral supplements may be harmful to your health. With a little planning you can obtain all the nutrients you need, the *Eat Well, Be Well*® way—as breakfast, lunch and dinner.

Water

Of all the essential nutrients, water is the most critical. It is involved in all the chemical reactions in the body, including the release of energy from food. It carries all other nutrients throug' out the body and also carries away waste products.

Generally, the adult body requires about one quart of water for every 1,000 calories of food eaten, or about six to eight glassfuls a day. That amount includes water found in other beverages and in foods. Most fruits and vegetables are about 80–90 percent water, and even bread is about 30 percent water by weight. Of course, the weather and our activity level also influence our water requirements.

The body's control mechanism for ensuring an adequate water intake is thirst, and it should never be ignored. Inadequate replacement of water can result in dehydration, heatstroke and death.

Folklore to the contrary, there is no nutritionally sound reason to avoid drinking water or other beverages with meals.

Fiber

Fiber (often called roughage) is the part of food that cannot be digested by enzymes in the digestive tract. The amount of fiber found in food is often expressed as "crude fiber," a scientific measurement of the organic material left after chemical digestion of food in the laboratory. But this process digests much more than the natural digestion that takes place in the body, so dietary fiber, which is usually two to five times higher than crude fiber, is the preferred measure.

Dietary fiber is only found in plant food such as fruits, vegetables, beans and grains. Different plants contain different types and amounts of fiber and different types of fiber act in different ways, so it is important to get your dietary fiber from a wide variety of foods.

Fiber is desirable in a balanced diet because it holds water, and in doing so, provides bulk to help the large intestine efficiently carry away body wastes. Diets that lack adequate amounts of fiber often cause constipation. On the other hand, excessive intakes of fiber can tie up important minerals and prevent their absorption by the body. A Recommended Dietary Allowance for fiber has not been established.

Essential Nutrients...How Much Do We Need?

Although we all need the same nutrients, different people require different amounts depending on their age, sex, weight, level of activity, lifestyle and state of health. For this reason, the Food and Nutrition Board of the National Academy of Sciences, National Research Council, established different Recommended Dietary Allowances (RDAs) for each sex and for a wide variety of age groups. These recommendations are based on continuous review of current research and knowledge in nutrition. They are revised about every five years.

The RDAs are the level of essential nutrients considered to be adequate to meet the known needs of practically all healthy persons. The allowances are well-above minimum requirements. The RDAs include a "margin of safety" that produces "reserve" body stores which are adequate for protection for weeks of low nutrient intake. Thus, the RDA amounts generally exceed each day's need by a significant margin.

All essential nutrients are not listed in the RDA tables. Current research suggests that if your daily diet contains adequate amounts of the nutrients for which recommendations are given, your diet will also contain adequate amounts of unlisted nutrients.

The RDAs are presented as guidelines to daily allowances for all healthy Americans. They do not mean that *you* must eat the recommended allowance for every nutrient every day. For example, extra amounts of a nutrient on one day during a week can compensate for shortages of that nutrient on another day. Just aim at getting adequate amounts of all nutrients over the course of a week.

A Simple Guide to an Adequate Diet

Analyzing your diet and comparing it to the RDA is a somewhat complicated way to be sure you are getting the nutrients you need, so the U.S. Department of Agriculture has done this analysis for you. It has simplified meal planning by incorporating both the nutrient needs of individuals and nutritive values of foods into a classification system called the Basic Four Food Groups. Each group contains a variety of foods with similar nutrient content. The recommended serving sizes for foods within each group supply similar amounts of major nutrients. Thus, you can ensure an adequate intake of all nutrients by eating the recommended number of servings from each of the four groups. In the following pages the Basic Four are described in detail. The table on the next page provides a summary of the groups with their serving sizes.

The Basic Four Food Groups

It's important to realize that although these servings are similar in nutrient content, they do not contain the same amount of calories. In some cases, the serving sizes are not typical. For example, 1½ cups of ice cream is needed to supply the same amount of calcium as an 8-ounce glass of milk, but this amount of ice cream is much more than a typical serving and would add more than 2½ times

The Basic Four Food Groups

Vegetable and Fruit Group

Servings per day: 4, including one good vitamin C source like oranges or orange juice and one deep-yellow or dark-green vegetable

Food	Amount per serving*
Vegetables, cut up	½ cup
Fruits, cut up	½ cup
Grapefruit	½ medium
Melon	½ medium
Orange	1
Potato	1 medium
Salad	1 bowl
Lettuce	1 wedge

Bread and Cereal Group

Servings per day: 4, whole grain or enriched only, including at least one serving of whole grain

Food	Amount per serving*
Bread	1 slice
Cereal	½ to ¾ cup, cooked
Pasta	½ to ¾ cup, cooked
Rice	½ to ¾ cup, cooked
Dry cereal	1 ounce

Milk Group

Servings per day: Children 0–9 years: 2 to 3; Children 9–12 years: 3; Teens: 4; Adults: 2; Pregnant women: 3; Nursing mothers: 4

Food	Amount per serving*
Milk	8 ounces (1 cup)
Yogurt, plain	1 cup
Hard cheese	1¼ ounces
Cheese spread	2 ounces
Ice cream	1½ cups
Cottage cheese	2 cups

Meat Group

Servings per day: 2 (can be eaten as mixtures of animal and vegetable foods; if only vegetable protein is consumed, it must be balanced)

Food	Amount per serving*
Meat, lean	2 to 3 ounces, cooked
Poultry	2 to 3 ounces, cooked
Fish	2 to 3 ounces, cooked
Eggs	2 to 3
Dry beans and peas	1 to 1½ cups cooked
Nuts and seeds	½ to ¾ cup
Peanut butter	4 tablespoons

*These amounts were established by the U.S. Department of Agriculture to meet specific nutritional requirements. For the milk group, serving sizes are based on the calcium content of 1 cup of milk. For the meat group, serving size is determined by protein content. Thus, rather than eat 2 cups of cottage cheese (milk group) or 4 tablespoons of peanut butter (meat group), it would make more sense to eat half those amounts and count each as half a serving in their respective groups.

the calories of a glass of whole milk or more than 4 times the calories of a glass of skim milk. Included within the description of each group is a section called "Best Bets for Waist Watchers," to help those who are counting calories. The foods listed within this section are the ones that deliver the most nutrients at the lowest caloric cost. These "Best Bets" are also the best choices for those watching their intake of fat, cholesterol and sugar.

A diet with the minimum number of servings suggested by the Basic Four plan furnishes about 1,200 calories—a good diet goal for those trying to lose weight. If your caloric needs are greater, you can choose extra servings from the Basic Four and/or choose foods from the USDA's fifth food group, "Fats, Sweets and Alcohol," which includes foods like butter, salad dressings, soft drinks and rich desserts. These foods are not included in any of the basic four groups because they supply calories but contribute little or no protein, vitamins or minerals to the diet. This does not mean that these foods are "bad" or "junk" foods. Rather they are extras to be enjoyed in moderation *after* you have met your nutrient needs with the proper servings of the Basic Four.

Vegetable and Fruit Group

Which Foods?

All fruits and vegetables (fresh, canned, frozen or dried) and their juices.

How Many Servings?

Plan an average of four servings from this group daily, including a good vitamin C source, and, at least three or four times a week, a good source of vitamin A.

What's a Serving?

Count one-half cup as a serving, or a typical portion—one orange, half a medium grapefruit, an apple, a small banana, a wedge of lettuce, a bowl of salad or a medium potato.

What's in It for You?

This group provides vitamins A, C, thiamine (B1), B6 and fiber, although individual foods in this group vary widely in how much of these they provide. Dark green and deep yellow-orange vegetables, such as apricots and cantaloupe, are good sources of vitamin A. Vitamin C comes particularly from citrus fruits (oranges, grapefruit, tangerines, lemons, limes, kumquats and ugli fruit), melons,

14

berries, tomatoes and dark green vegetables, if not overcooked. Most dark green vegetables also contribute riboflavin (B2), folacin, iron and magnesium, and certain greens—collards, kale, mustard, turnip and dandelion—provide calcium as well. All fruits and vegetables, except avocados and olives, contain little or no fat, and none contain the cholesterol found in meats and dairy products. Unpeeled fruits and vegetables and those with edible seeds (strawberries, blackberries, kiwi) are particularly good sources of fiber.

Best Bets for Waist Watchers

Fruits and vegetables can be a dieter's best friends. They offer a variety of nutrients without excessive calories. Experiment with the wide variety of colorful vegetables to add zest and interest to your meals, but try to steer clear of high calorie sauces and toppings, and choose cooking methods that don't require added fat.

Fresh fruits can satisfy an urge for sweetness. But remember, fruits and fruit juices do have calories, so, if you are a serious calorie counter, keep portion sizes moderate. Choose fresh, unsweetened frozen, and juice-packed canned fruits, instead of those in heavy syrups.

Bread and Cereal Group

Which Foods?

All foods made from whole grain or enriched flour or meal. This group includes bread, biscuits, muffins, waffles, pancakes, cereals, cornmeal, flour, grits, rolled oats, barley, pasta, rice, bulgur, kasha and tortillas.

How Many Servings?

An average of four servings daily for everyone.

What's a Serving?

One small muffin, roll, pancake, waffle or a slice of bread; one-half of an English muffin, bagel or hamburger or frankfurter bun; ½ to ¾ cup cooked cereal, cornmeal, grits, pasta or rice; one ounce ready-to-eat cereal.

What's in It for You?

These foods are good sources of iron, thiamine, niacin (B3) and riboflavin (B2) and they provide some protein. Whole-grain products also contribute vitamin E, folacin and B6, as well as magnesium, zinc, copper and fiber, so it's a good idea to include some of these less refined varieties in your diet.

Most breakfast cereals are fortified to contain higher levels of nutrients than those in natural grain products. In fact, some of these cereals are also fortified with vitamins not usually found in grain products, such as vitamins A, B12, C and D.

Best Bets for Waist Watchers

Opt for low-calorie choices by selecting products that have no sugar or other sweeteners added and little or no fat. Also skip the spreads, sauces, gravies and toppings. Although such items such as pastries, cakes and cookies are considered to be in the bread group if they are made with enriched flour, they have more calories per serving than the usual breads and rolls. Pita bread, matzo and many flat breads are excellent choices because they are usually made without fat. Most granola cereals are higher in calories than other types, because they contain fats (usually saturated coconut oil or hydrogenated vegetable oils) as well as sweeteners (sugar, brown sugar or honey). Read labels.

Milk and Cheese Group

Which Foods?

All types of milk, cheese, yogurt, ice cream and ice milk.

How Many Servings?

Children under 9	2 to 3 servings
Children 9–12	3 servings
Teens	4 servings
Adults	2 servings
Pregnant women	3 servings
Nursing mothers	4 servings

What's a Serving?

Count 8 ounces of milk (whole, low-fat or skim) as a serving. Serving sizes of dairy products are based on their calcium content—not typical portion sizes—and they are not equal in calories or protein content. Some examples of the serving sizes that contain the same amount of calcium as one cup of milk are:

1 cup yogurt
2-inch cube (about 1¼ ounces) hard cheese

16

4 tablespoons (2 ounces) processed cheese spread
2 ounces processed cheese food
4 tablespoons grated parmesan cheese
2 cups cottage cheese
1½ cups ice cream or ice milk

Don't forget to count the milk and cheese used in cooked foods (cream soups, sauces and puddings) toward meeting your daily quota in this group.

What's in It for You?

Milk and milk products are the major sources of calcium in the American diet. This group also provides generous amounts of high-quality protein and vitamins A, B6, B12 and riboflavin. Additionally, dairy products are often fortified with vitamin D.

A diet that is severely restricted in milk and milk products may not supply adequate calcium—a nutrient that is needed throughout the lifecycle. A lack of calcium in the diet may contribute to the development of osteoporosis, a condition in which the bones become brittle and break easily. This disease is most common among postmenopausal women but has its roots in the teen years and young adulthood when bones are reaching their maximum strength and mass.

Some people have problems digesting the sugar in milk (lactose) and therefore avoid all milk products. But lactose intolerant people can sometimes tolerate yogurt and certain cheeses without problem and can even drink milk if they keep portion sizes small (4 to 6 ounces) or add commercial lactase to it. If you think you have an intolerance to milk products, consult your doctor.

Best Bets for Waist Watchers

Keep calories in check by choosing skim or low-fat milk and yogurt. They all provide the same nutrients as their whole milk counterparts, but contain less fat and cholesterol and fewer calories. Wise choices are:

nonfat-dry milk
skim milk
1% low-fat milk
buttermilk (skim or low-fat)
evaporated skim milk
low-fat cottage cheese
low-fat cheeses such as baker's cheese, farmer's
cheese, part-skim ricotta, low-fat mozzarella, low-fat
processed cheeses, and some goat cheeses

Meat, Poultry, Fish and Bean Group

Which Foods?

Beef, veal, lamb, pork, poultry, fish, shellfish, organ meats, eggs, dried peas and beans, seeds, nuts, peanuts and peanut butter.

How Many Servings?

An average of two servings daily are recommended from this group.

What's a Serving?

Two to three ounces of lean, cooked meat, poultry or fish (all without bone).

The following portions can substitute for *one* ounce of meat, fish or poultry.

  1 egg
  ½ to ¾ cup cooked dry beans or peas
  2 tablespoons peanut butter
  ¼ to ½ cup nuts, sesame seeds or sunflower seeds

What's in It for You?

The foods in this group are especially valued for their protein content, but they are also good sources of iron, zinc, phosphorus and B6. Animal protein foods also supply vitamin B12. Choosing a variety of foods within this group is especially important, as each has distinct nutritional advantages. For example, red meats and oysters are rich sources of zinc. Liver and egg yolks are valuable sources of vitamin A. Dried peas and beans are good sources of magnesium and fiber and are very low in fat.

Best Bets for Waist Watchers

When selecting and preparing meats, choose lean cuts or varieties, trim all visible fats, and broil, bake or roast without added fat. Good choices include:

Beef:	flank steak, round steak, ground round, rump roast
Veal:	all cuts except breast
Lamb:	leg or loin
Pork:	loin chop, tenderloin, sirloin roast
Poultry:	chicken or turkey without skin
Game:	venison, rabbit
Fish:	flounder, sole, cod, ocean perch, turbot, haddock, pollack. (All fresh fish are relatively low in calories.)

Shellfish: all types (shrimp contain more cholesterol than other varieties, but, like the other types, are relatively low in fat.)

Dried peas and beans and eggs (if you're not on a low cholesterol diet) are also good choices for the calorie-conscious.

The "Extra" Group: Fats, Sweets and Alcohol

Which Foods?

Butter, margarine, mayonnaise, salad dressings, other fats and oils and olives; candy, sugar, honey, molasses, jams, jellies, syrups, sweet toppings and other concentrated sweets; soft drinks, fruit punches and other highly sugared beverages; alcoholic beverages such as wine, beer and liquor; and refined but unenriched breads, pastries and flour products. Bacon, cream, sour cream, cream cheese· and other foods are also often included in this group because they are very high in fat.

How Many Servings?

No basic number of servings is suggested for this group. These foods can be used in moderation to round out meals as long as requirements of the other categories are met. Some of these foods are used as ingredients in prepared foods or are added to other foods at the table. Others are just "extras."

What's a Serving?

No serving size is defined.

What's in It for You?

These foods provide relatively few nutrients in proportion to the number of calories they contain. Vegetable oils generally supply vitamin E and essential fatty acids, but a little goes a long way toward meeting your needs. Most of this "other" food group are extras to be added, as your calorie allotment permits, for improved taste and enjoyment.

What About....

Most of the problems with the American diet today result from excess, not deficiency. But these problems can be eliminated by practicing the three basic principles of healthful eating—*moderation, variety* and *balance.*

Moderation

Just as you need an adequate amount of essential nutrients for good health, too much of any vitamin, mineral, carbohydrate, fat, protein or fiber can be harmful. Thus, moderation is a key word in a healthful diet. Eating is, and should be, one of the pleasures of life. Fortunately, it is rarely necessary to completely forego the foods you love. For example, a hot-fudge sundae once a month can be a harmless treat; but a hot fudge sundae every day instead of lunch is unwise. That choice would provide too much fat and sugar calories while short-changing you on other important nutrients.

Moderation also means watching portion sizes. Moderate portions will not only help keep calories under control, but will also lead to the second principle of good nutrition—eating a wide variety of foods.

Variety

No single food contains all the essential nutrients in just the amounts needed for good health, so eating a wide variety of food is the key for obtaining enough—but not too much—of every kind of nutrient. Success with the Basic Four depends on variety. Although the foods in each of the four groups contain similar patterns of key nutrients, the nutritive value of the foods within each group varies. Variety *among* the four food groups ensures the adequacy of certain key nutrients, and variety *within* each group ensures an adequate intake of all other nutrients.

Let's look at an example. Within the Bread and Cereal Group, both whole grain and enriched refined products are good sources of some B vitamins and iron. But eating only refined, enriched products—white bread, white rice, white flour—may leave you short in fiber and certain trace minerals that were partially removed in the milling process. On the other hand, eating only very high fiber foods such as bran products, may provide excessive amounts of fiber. Too much fiber can interfere with the absorption of minerals such as iron and zinc.

The answer, of course, is *variety*. The greater the variety both among and within food groups, the less likely you are to develop either a deficiency or an excess of any single nutrient. Variety also reduces the chance of being exposed to too much of any of the natural or added chemical substances in food.

Balance

Eating moderate amounts of a wide variety of foods automatically leads to the third key to good nutrition—*balance*. A balanced diet contains foods from each of the four food groups. However, even a diet containing highly nutritious foods is not balanced if all of the food groups are not represented in the proper amounts. Consequently, fad diets with a great emphasis on certain foods or certain nutrients, such as protein, are unhealthy. These diets are nutritionally unbalanced—often dangerously so. Similarly, too much of a nutritious food can unbalance a diet because it may crowd out foods from the other food groups.

Eating a balanced diet also means balancing energy intake—how much you eat—against energy expenditure—how much you exercise—so as to achieve and maintain an appropriate body weight.

In short, an adequate diet provides an appropriate *balance* of nutrients from *moderate* portions of a *variety* of foods from each of the Basic Four Food Groups.

II
Dietary
Guidelines
for
Americans

Dietary Guidelines

In February 1980, the U.S. Departments of Agriculture and Health and Human Services established seven Dietary Guidelines for Americans based on moderation, variety and balance as the keys to healthful eating habits. These guidelines are useful adjuncts to the Basic Four Food Groups and the Recommended Dietary Allowances because they focus on nutritional excesses in the diet (overnutrition) rather than nutritional needs.

A second edition of the Dietary Guidelines—very similar to the 1980 edition—was published by these departments in 1985. The revised version of the guidelines continues to reflect the basic rules of moderation, variety and balance, as explained in the following sections.

Eat a Variety of Foods

Nutrition scientists agree that good overall nutrition is a necessary component of good health, and that the basis of good nutrition is eating a moderate amount of a wide variety of foods from the Basic Four Food Groups. Variety minimizes the possibility of excesses and maximizes the likelihood of obtaining all necessary nutrients. Good nutrition, without excesses or deficiencies, is the primary goal of the *Eat Well, Be Well*® food plan.

Maintain Desirable Weight

Obesity is the most serious nutritional problem in the United States, affecting about 14 percent of men and 24 percent of women. People who exceed their desirable weight by 10 to 20 percent are usually classified as overweight; those whose weight exceeds 20 percent of their desirable weight are termed obese.

There are definite health risks associated with being overweight. Excessive weight appears to bring out latent adult-onset diabetes and latent high blood pressure, and is also associated with increased levels of blood fats and cholesterol. All of these, in turn, are associated with an increased risk of heart attack and stroke. Other health hazards associated with or aggravated by obesity include gallbladder disorders, gynecological irregularities, arthritis, varicose veins, gout, cancer of the breast, colon, uterus and prostate, postsurgical complications, difficulties during pregnancy and kidney disorders.

Because of these and other problems, an obese person statistically has 50 percent more chance of dying than a person of similar age but normal weight. However, all, or almost all, of the ill effects of obesity can be reversed. Often, simple weight reduction can bring blood pressure down to a satisfactory level and get diabetes under control. Life insurance studies show that those who successfully lose weight—and keep it off—bring their life expectancy back to what it would have been if they had never been obese.

Although those people whose weight is 10 percent or more *below* their desirable weight don't face the health risks associated with obesity, they are subject to other health problems that are not yet clearly understood. It is very important that underweight individuals get a thorough physical examination by a physician to make sure that failure to gain weight, or the sudden loss of weight, is not the result of a medical problem. (For more advice on controlling your weight, see Chapters III and IV.)

Avoid Too Much Fat, Saturated Fat, and Cholesterol

Although a moderate amount of fat is needed in everyone's diet, many people go overboard. The fat content of the average American diet has increased from 32 percent of total calories in 1910 to about 40 percent at present. Approximately 15–17 percent of total calories now comes from saturated fats, primarily from meat and meat products, dairy products and some saturated vegetable oils (coconut oil, palm oil and hydrogenated oils).

Our high-fat eating habits may cause problems in two ways. First, fat is a very concentrated energy source, supplying more than twice the calories per gram of protein or carbohydrate. An excess of fat in the diet can mean excess calories and extra pounds.

Second, although levels of blood cholesterol vary among individuals, populations such as ours with a high-fat diet—especially a diet high in saturated fat and cholesterol—often have higher levels of cholesterol in the blood. Higher levels of blood cholesterol are generally associated with a greater risk of developing heart disease. Based on this association, some nutrition scientists and health and government agencies recommend that all Americans reduce their fat intake to 30–35 percent of their total calories (with saturated fats making up no more than a third of this) and limit their intake of cholesterol to 300 milligrams each day.

Other scientists, however, feel that there is not sufficient scientific evidence to warrant such a broad recommendation. They argue that there is a tremendous variation in the individual response to dietary fat and cholesterol. This view sees an elevated blood cholesterol, which is a risk factor for the development of heart disease, as only moderately related to dietary cholesterol. Instead, high blood cholesterol is more related to saturated fat, total number of calories eaten and to genetic factors. Thus, some people can consume diets high in saturated fats and cholesterol and maintain normal blood cholesterol levels, while others will have high blood cholesterol levels even if they eat a low-fat, low-cholesterol diet.

Whichever view you take, avoiding too much fat and cholesterol is a prudent course to follow. But alone it is no guarantee against heart disease, nor can it compensate for other coronary risk factors such as cigarette smoking,* obesity, hypertension or lack of exercise. No diet can take the place of regular checkups with your physician evaluating your blood cholesterol status.

Both cholesterol and dietary fat play an essential role in nutrition and neither are villains in *moderation*. Health concerns associated with them are related to either inadequate or excessive use. Unless your doctor has recommended otherwise, you should include moderate use of nutritious foods like meat, eggs and dairy products in your diet despite their fat and cholesterol contents. These foods are rich sources of many essential vitamins and minerals as well as protein.

The *Eat Well, Be Well*® recipes provide delicious ways to eat well and keep dietary fat within recommended levels. Other advice for cutting excess fat out of your diet can be found on pages 66–68.

Eat Foods with Adequate Starch and Fiber

As explained earlier, carbohydrates include sugars (simple carbohydrates) and starches (complex carbohydrates). The Dietary Guidelines recommend that you eat adequate amounts of complex carbohydrate foods such as legumes, fruits and vegetables, enriched and whole grain breads, cereals and pasta. These foods are excellent choices because they are economical and contain many essential nutrients. Because carbohydrates have less than half the calories of fat, countries where most people eat high carbohydrate diets show a lower proportion of obesity and health problems related to obesity.

Increasing your consumption of certain complex carbohydrates can also help you increase dietary fiber. Dietary fiber provides the bulk to move waste through your digestive system faster, so eating more foods high in fiber tends to reduce the symptoms of chronic constipation, diverticulosis and hemorrhoids.

The possible role of high fiber diets in helping to prevent cardiovascular disease and cancer of the colon and in treating diabetes is under study.

*Almost a third of heart disease fatalities have been related to smoking.

The best way to ensure adequate amounts of starch and fiber in your diet is to eat, as recommended, four portions of fruits and vegetables and four portions of breads, cereals and other grain products (including whole grains) each day. Adding fiber supplements to an unbalanced diet will do little or no good and can be harmful. Excessive fiber can cause excess gas and bloating, intestinal obstruction and other conditions. It can also reduce the absorption of essential vitamins and minerals.

Suggestions for increasing fiber intake can be found on pages 33–34.

Avoid Too Much Sugar

Sugars are simple carbohydrates that are used by the body for energy. Many of the foods you eat every day contain some form of natural sugar. Most of these foods, such as fruits, vegetables, grains and milk, are also richly endowed with other nutrients. But the most commonly eaten sugar—sucrose—and other caloric sweeteners, such as corn syrup or honey, offer little nutrition except calories. In fact, they unbalance the diet by replacing other foods that offer vitamins, minerals and protein in addition to energy.

The major health hazard from eating too much sugar is tooth decay, but this risk of dental cavities is not simply a matter of how much sugar you eat. Cavities are caused by the acid produced from bacteria feeding on carbohydrates in the mouth. Any fermentable carbohydrate, including starch, can be turned into cavity-promoting acid by the bacteria in the mouth. The amount of sugar or other carbohydrate in a food is less important in the development of tooth decay than the frequency of eating it and length of time the carbohydrate food remains in contact with the teeth. Between-meal sweets that remain in the mouth (such as hard candies) and sticky sweets (such as taffy, caramel and some "health food" bars) are the most likely to cause cavities.

Contrary to popular belief, sugar does not cause diabetes or cardio-vascular disease. Any alleged relationship between excess sugar and these diseases boils down to their relationship to being overweight. Becoming overweight is caused by eating too many calories, regardless of whether those calories come from the sugar bowl, a steak or avocados.

A moderate intake of sugar can add to the pleasure of eating with no nutrition threat. But the amount of sugar that you can eat and still maintain a balanced diet depends on your energy requirements. Remember that added sugar and rich desserts should be eaten as "extras" and should not take the place of foods from the Basic Four with more nutrients.

To learn how to avoid excess sugar calories, turn to pages 68–69.

Avoid Too Much Sodium

Sodium is an essential dietary mineral. It is crucial to fluid balance in the body, aids in the absorption of nutrients across the cell walls, and plays an important role in transmitting nerve impulses to the muscles.

As vital as sodium is, there's a good chance you're eating much more than your body actually requires. Sodium comes into the diet from several sources, but the most common source is *table salt*—or sodium chloride, which is 40 percent sodium.

Physiologically, our bodies need only about 200 milligrams of sodium a day—the amount found in about one-tenth of a teaspoon of salt. But most Americans consume 2,300 to 6,900 milligrams of sodium daily (about 1 to 3 teaspoons of salt), which is twice the range that the National Research Council suggests as a "safe and adequate" level.

If you are thinking that you don't add this much salt to your food every day, you're probably right. If you're a typical American only about one-third of the sodium you eat comes from your salt shaker or other salt-containing seasonings added in cooking or at the table. Approximately another third occurs naturally in food and in water, and the remainder of the sodium in your diet comes from packaged foods in which salt and other sodium compounds are added for flavor or as preservatives.

A healthy body can generally tolerate large amounts of extra sodium, so most of us have no problem with our sodium intakes.

But for people who have high blood pressure (hypertension), excess sodium is a major hazard. Untreated hypertension is the leading cause of strokes in the United States, and is a major contributor to heart attacks, heart failure and kidney failure. Approximately 20 percent of all American adults have (or will develop) high blood pressure, and one-third of these individuals will be particularly sensitive to sodium's effects. For this susceptible population, excess salt *can* elevate blood pressure in those who already have hypertension and *may* increase the risk of developing hypertension for people who are genetically susceptible to the disease and are particularly sensitive to salt.

27

At present, it is not possible to predict who will develop high blood pressure, so many health professionals are recommending that all Americans practice moderation in their sodium intake. Cutting down on excessive salt intake is not known to be dangerous or harmful and may be beneficial to those who have inherited the tendency to become hypertensive.

Recent research suggests that inadequate quantities of other nutrients, such as calcium, potassium and magnesium, may also have an effect on the development of hypertension. Therefore, it is important that you do not eliminate or severely restrict your intake of any highly nutritious foods or food group unless your doctor has prescribed a strict low-sodium diet for you.

The exact cause of essential hypertension (the most common form) is still unknown. But the disorder is complex involving many elements. For instance, blacks and those who have a family history of hypertension have a higher frequency of the disease, and there is a definite link between obesity and high blood pressure. Many overweight people who develop hypertension can reduce, and often normalize, their blood pressure just by losing weight.

For these reasons, regardless of your diet, you should have your blood pressure checked on a regular basis. High blood pressure often has no noticeable symptoms, so you could have it and not even know it. If your blood pressure is high, follow your doctor's advice regarding diet and/or medication. For ways to reduce the sodium content of your diet, see pages 35–36.

If You Drink Alcoholic Beverages, Do So in Moderation

Alcohol is a central nervous system depressant that affects every organ in the body. It can affect nutritional status in several ways. Alcohol contains a lot of calories—seven calories per gram—but virtually no other nutrients. And adding anything except club soda, seltzer, diet soda or water to the alcohol, increases the calories in your drink even further.

These extra calories may not be a problem for the active person with a high total calorie allowance, but budgeting alcohol calories into a balanced reducing diet can be difficult. Heavy drinkers can quickly develop a serious nutritional handicap, since "empty" alcohol calories usually make up a good part of their daily caloric intake, taking the place of food, with more nutrients. Alcohol also increases the body's needs for certain B vitamins while impairing its ability to absorb and utilize these and other nutrients.

Excessive consumption of alcoholic beverages by pregnant women may cause birth defects or other problems during pregnancy. The level of consumption at which risks to the unborn occur has not been established. Therefore, the National Institute on Alcohol Abuse and Alcoholism advises that pregnant women should refrain from the use of alcohol.

Good nutrition can help the body handle alcohol, but it can't protect against the many serious conditions caused by chronic heavy drinking, so *moderation* is an essential factor for attaining and maintaining good health. One to two drinks daily appear to cause no harm in adults who enjoy a social drink on occasion or a glass of wine with dinner. But it is important that the calories in alcoholic beverages not replace food from the Basic Four Food Groups.

If you would like to cut down on the amount of alcohol in your diet, see page 69 for some helpful tips.

Remember that the seven Dietary Guidelines for Americans are not hard-and-fast rules, but are just guidelines designed to improve the health of Americans by stressing good eating habits. They do not recommend the exclusion of any specific food or food group. It is also important to be aware that a guideline that reads "avoid too much sugar" does not necessarily mean "eat less sugar," nor does "eat adequate fiber" necessarily mean "eat more fiber." People differ and their food needs and intakes differ.

Nutrition scientists are still searching for the role, if any, of specific nutrients in chronic conditions such as heart disease, high blood pressure, diabetes and some types of cancer. But evidence is growing that diet does play a role in some nondietary diseases. Obesity, for example, is known to worsen or contribute to the development of several degenerative diseases.

Therefore, the basis of all the Dietary Guidelines, and of most responsible nutrition advice regarding anticancer diets, antiheart disease diets, and weight-loss diets is still moderation, variety and balance. By enjoying a *variety* of foods in *moderate* amounts from the Basic Four Food Groups, you can easily obtain all of the nutrients essential to good health and avoid an excessively high intake of any potentially undesirable dietary component.

Is Your Diet a Perfect "10?"

How well does your present diet reflect the basics of good nutrition? Before you answer, take the following quiz. It will help you determine how closely your eating habits follow the Dietary Guidelines.

1. **Do you eat at least two servings of vegetables every day?**

    _____ Yes _____ No

    Put a check next to those foods listed below that you usually eat during the week:

_____	green beans	_____	beets
_____	corn	_____	carrots
_____	green or tossed salad	_____	cauliflower
_____	broccoli	_____	asparagus
_____	Brussels sprouts	_____	spinach, kale, collard greens
_____	mushrooms	_____	cabbage
_____	turnips, rutabaga	_____	sprouts (alfalfa, bean)
_____	sweet potatoes	_____	winter squash (acorn, butternut)
_____	peas, pea pods		
_____	tomatoes	_____	other green vegetables
_____	sweet peppers	_____	other deep-yellow vegetables

2. **How many days a week is orange juice the only fruit you get in your diet?**

    _____

3. **Do you know your desirable weight?**

    _____ Yes _____ No

    If yes, how much more than desirable is your weight?

    _____ Less than 10% _____ 10–20% _____ Over 20%

4. **When on a diet, how much do you try to lose each week?**

    _____ 1–2 pounds _____ 3–5 pounds _____ Over 5 pounds

5. **When trying to lose weight, do you avoid breads, rolls, potatoes, pasta and other starchy foods?**

    _____ Yes _____ No

6. **Do you eat some whole grain products, nuts or legumes each day?**

    _____ Yes _____ No

    Check the foods below that you include in your diet throughout the week:

_____	whole grain breads or rolls	_____	whole grain cereal (bran, oatmeal, granola, wheat germ)
_____	whole grain muffins or crackers		
_____	whole grain pasta	_____	split peas or lentils
_____	tortillas or corn bread	_____	dried beans (black beans, kidney beans, pintos, garbanzos)
_____	brown rice		

_____ bulgur (cracked wheat)   _____ nuts

7. **Now let's take a look at the sources of fat in your diet. Do you usually:**

Yes No

_____ _____ Have eggs with bacon or sausage for breakfast every day?

_____ _____ Prefer cream or half-and-half in your coffee or tea and use only whole milk for drinking and cooking?

_____ _____ Eat meat for lunch and dinner every day?

_____ _____ Eat the visible fat on meats and the skin on poultry?

_____ _____ Use butter, oil, margarine or animal fat in the preparation of most dishes?

_____ _____ Fry many foods such as potatoes, steak, burgers, chicken or fish?

_____ _____ Add butter or margarine to cooked vegetables and to breads and rolls?

8. **How much sodium is in your diet? Do you usually:**

Yes No

_____ _____ Add salt to your food in cooking and at the table?

_____ _____ Eat canned vegetables instead of fresh or unseasoned frozen?

_____ _____ Eat canned or frozen entrees?

_____ _____ Rely heavily on commercially prepared bouillon, broth and soups for quick meals and in cooking?

_____ _____ Eat processed meats such as bologna, salami, pastrami, sausage, frankfurters and corned beef several times a week?

_____ _____ Snack on salted nuts, pretzels, potato chips, corn chips, pickles and olives?

_____ _____ Use condiments such as soy sauce, ketchup, mustard, garlic salt, onion salt, barbeque sauce, steak sauce or Worcestershire sauce to add flavor to food?

9. **Do you have a sweet tooth? Let's find out. Do you usually:**

Yes No

_____ _____ Add sugar or honey to coffee or tea?

_____ _____ Eat sweet desserts after meals?

_____ _____ Snack on sweets between meals?

_____ _____ Sip sodas or fruit drinks during the day?

_____ _____ Prefer sweet rolls, pastries and sugared cereals to whole grain breads and unsweetened cereals?

_____ _____ Chew sugared gum or eat hard candies between meals?

10. Do you usually drink more than one cocktail at lunch and dinner?

_____ Yes   _____ No

Rate Your Eating Habits

To find out if your diet is a perfect "10," read the 10 answers below.

Do you eat at least two servings of vegetables every day?

It's important to eat two or more servings of varied vegetables every day, not the same tossed salad or dish of green beans. Vegetables are excellent sources of many vitamins, minerals and fiber, but they often vary in the amounts and kinds of these nutrients they provide. For example, ½ cup of Brussels sprouts supplies more than 100 percent of the RDA for vitamin C, but contains less than 10 percent of the RDA for vitamin A. In contrast, ½ cup of carrots provides well over 100 percent of the RDA for vitamin A, but less than 10 percent of the recommended allowance for vitamin C.

Vegetables are also affected by how they're cooked. For maximum nutritional value, steam vegetables or boil in a small amount of water. Covering vegetables completely in water reduces both nutritional content and taste.

It is nutritionally better to eat moderate amounts of a wide variety of vegetables than the same two or three over and over again. If you checked five or more varieties from the given list, with at least two being dark-green or deep-yellow, you're probably getting a good balance of all the nutrients provided by vegetables.

How many days a week is orange juice the only fruit you get in your diet?

Your diet should contain more fruit than orange juice alone. Orange juice is an American favorite and it is an excellent source of vitamin C. But it does not contain as much vitamin A as canta-loupe, as much vitamin B6 as a banana or as much fiber as an apple. Eating a variety of fruits during the week will provide you with a better balance of nutrients in your diet.

Do you know your desirable weight?

If your present weight is more than the range suggested on the Metropolitan Height and Weight Tables (page 40), you may have a weight problem (especially if you are more than 10 percent over the suggested weight range). If you would like to take off a few pounds, or just stay at your present weight, be sure to read Chapters III and IV.

When on a diet, how much do you try to lose each week?

The safest, most sensible and most effective diet plan calls for a gradual weight loss of only one or two pounds per week. Contrary to the false claims of "miracle" fad diets, you can't lose weight overnight without risking your health. Be patient. Pounds lost quickly tend to represent water loss, but pounds lost gradually tend to be fat and are more likely to stay off. Unlike most fad plans, a gradual weight loss diet allows enough food to provide the essential nutrients you need for good health. You'll feel better and find it easier to stick with the diet.

For a more complete discussion on the problems of fad diets, see the section on "Miracle Diets and Magic Pills" (pages 50–54).

When trying to lose weight, do you avoid breads, rolls, potatoes, pasta and other starchy foods?

You'll be better off nutritionally if you can answer "no" to this important question. Many people who watch their weight have the misconception that breads, potatoes, pasta and the like are taboo on a diet, but the fact is that these foods are nutritious, inexpensive, filling and less fattening than many other foods. In fact, the fat content of these "starchy" foods is virtually zero, and fat contains more than twice the calories of carbohydrate or protein. A medium baked potato for example has about 100 calories, but add a couple of heaping tablespoons of sour cream, which is high in fat, and you instantly double the calories. A slice of bread is a low 65 calories until you add a 35-calorie pat of butter and a 40-calorie packet of jam. Have a half cup of noodles for a slim 100 calories, or add a cream sauce and up the calorie total to almost 300.

Of course, you can't eat unlimited quantities of starchy foods without piling on the calories, but, in moderation, these complex carbohydrate foods are great diet foods. Become familiar with the number of calories in various foods from the bread and cereal group so that you can adjust your intake accordingly. Skip the high-calorie sauces, gravies, spreads and toppings, and remember to watch your portion sizes.

Do you eat some whole grain products, nuts or legumes each day?

Whole grains, nuts and legumes are excellent sources of fiber (roughage). Adequate fiber in the diet is necessary for proper digestion and elimination.

The list of foods under question 6 are all good sources of fiber that are often overlooked. If you checked at least three foods from this list, not only are you getting fiber, vitamins, minerals and some protein, but you are also practicing variety in your diet. There are many different types of fiber and each has different properties. It's important not to try to get all of your fiber from just one high-fiber food such as bran. And remember that too much fiber can lead to gastrointestinal problems and poor nutrient absorption.

If you feel that your fiber intake is too low, here are a few ways to boost the fiber content of your diet:

If you usually eat enriched white bread, add variety with whole wheat or rye selections. Rolled oats, wheat bran, wheat germ and whole grain flours will add fiber and a robust, nutlike flavor to home-baked breads and muffins.

Change from low-fiber breakfast cereals such as cornflakes to whole grain or bran cereals.

Several times a week, substitute brown rice, bulgur (cracked wheat) or a dried bean dish for potatoes, enriched pasta or rice.

Include the recommended four servings from the fruit and vegetable group each day and eat fruits unpeeled whenever possible.

Make the switch from low-fiber to high-fiber foods gradually to prevent digestive problems; and because fiber absorbs water, drink plenty of liquids as you increase your fiber intake.

Now let's take a look at the sources of fat in your diet.

If "yes" was your answer to quite a few of the choices in question 7, you may be eating more fat than the Dietary Guidelines recommend. There is a tremendous variation in the response of individuals to dietary fat (and cholesterol), but for many Americans, excess fat is a source of unneeded and, therefore, unhealthy calories.

If you would like to cut down on the amount of fat in your diet, here are some suggestions to get you started.

Put some low-fat variety on your breakfast plate by skipping the high-cholesterol, high-fat eggs and bacon in favor of cereal with skim milk, cottage cheese with fruit or pancakes with a fruit topping.

Select low-fat or skim milk and skim milk products often; use cream, sour cream and half-and-half only occasionally.

Instead of having meat at every meal, add variety to your diet with nonmeat main courses such as fish, vegetable casseroles, or a dish made with dried peas or beans.

Trim excess fat from meats and remove skin from chicken before cooking or eating.

Cook without added fat or use only small amounts of fat whenever possible. To reduce the saturated fat and cholesterol in your diet, choose soft margarines or vegetable oils instead of butter, hydrogenated vegetable shortenings, lard, salt pork or chicken fat.

Roast, bake, broil, poach or steam instead of frying.

Season cooked vegetables with herbs, spices or lemon juice rather than with heavy sauces, butter or margarine and cut out or reduce the amount of butter or margarine you spread on breads.

How much sodium is in your diet?

Did you often find yourself checking "yes" to the questions about your sodium intake? If you did, you're probably eating much more sodium than your body needs. This extra sodium may be no problem for you, but if you think that you should moderate your intake, here are some hints to make it easier:

Gradually reduce the amount of salt you add to food during cooking and try not to add any at the table.

Use more fresh or plain frozen vegetables and cut back on the canned or seasoned frozen varieties, which have salt added.

Use fresh meats, poultry and fish and make your own mixed dishes, instead of relying heavily on frozen or canned main dishes, which can contain at least 1,000 milligrams of sodium or more per serving.

Most canned and dehydrated soups contain 800 to 1,300 milligrams of sodium in an 8-ounce serving. Substitute homemade soups made with fresh ingredients or look for the new sodium-reduced soups.

Sausages, luncheon meats, frankfurters and canned meats contain large amounts of sodium (250 to 450 milligrams per ounce) because salt is generally added as a preservative during processing. In contrast, fresh meats, fish and poultry contain only 15–25 milligrams of sodium per ounce.

Limit the use of salty snack foods such as salted nuts and popcorn, potato chips, corn chips, pretzels and pickles. Look for the unsalted varieties of these foods.

Condiments such as the ones listed in question 8 can really run the sodium count up even when they are eaten with a naturally low-sodium food, so make only sparing use of these extras. Try flavoring your food with a pinch of a zesty herb and reach for wine, vinegar or lemon juice instead of salt seasonings when making marinades, salad dressings and sauces. (See page 85 for a helpful guide to herbs and spices.)

Read food labels and learn to recognize ingredients that contain sodium (see page 194).

Remember that even if you are trying to reduce the sodium in your diet, it is still important to select a balanced variety of foods from each of the Basic Four every day.

If you would like information on how much sodium is in particular food items, a helpful publication is "The Sodium Content of Your Food" (Home & Garden Bulletin 233), which can be purchased from the Superintendent of Documents, U.S. Government Printing Office, Washington, DC 20402 for $2.25.

Do you have a sweet tooth?

If you often answered "yes" to the list in question 9, chances are that you have a sweet tooth. If you do, you'll be glad to know that just because sugar tastes good doesn't mean that it's bad for you. Sugar is itself a carbohydrate nutrient because it supplies energy, and you may need the extra calories sugar adds to your diet if you are underweight or very active. But sugar contains no protein, vitamins or minerals, so sweets and sugary desserts can contribute to a nutrient-poor diet if they are eaten instead of foods that supply needed nutrients.

Sticky sweets eaten between meals can also contribute to tooth decay.

If you are watching your weight, eating less sugar is an easy way to decrease your caloric intake. Pages 68–69 provide many tips to help you find and cut back on excess sugar calories.

If you don't have a weight problem, but still prefer to eat less of sugar's "empty calories," look for sweet treats that have nutritional plus points such as *Eat Well, Be Well's* Baked Orange Pudding (page 174), Blueberry Yogurt Cream Pie (page 175), and Peanut Butter Raisin Cookies (page 180). These sweets count as dessert and count nutritionally, too.

Do you usually drink more than one cocktail at lunch and dinner?

If your answer to question 10 is "yes," your intake of alcohol may be more than what the Dietary Guidelines suggest is a moderate amount. People differ and a specific "safe" upper limit for alcohol intake is difficult to determine. However, one or two drinks daily appear to cause no harm in adults who do not have problems with alcohol. If you are pregnant, avoid all alcoholic beverages.

The type of alcoholic beverages you prefer can also make a difference. For example, a double martini has almost four times the alcohol content of a glass of dry wine.

Alcohol certainly isn't a necessary part of the daily meal plan. But if you drink, be sure that your intake of alcoholic beverages is consistent with your health and nutritional goals.

If you decide you would like to reduce the number of calories you get from alcohol-containing beverages, see "Cutting Alcohol Calories," page 69.

How did you do?

Is your diet a perfect "10?" If you're like most of us, it's probably not. Good nutrition, however, is not really a matter of yes or no, right or wrong, black or white. It's a matter of balance, variety and moderation. The quiz supplies simple guidelines to help you rate your eating habits and plan for improvement. But don't think that you have to revamp your entire eating repertoire overnight. Drastic changes aren't necessary—moderation is usually the solution to most dietary problems.

III
Weight Control —A Matter of Balance

How Does Your Weight Rate?

The Mirror Test

What kind of shape are you in? A good look in a full-length mirror without your clothing will give you a clue. Look at yourself from the side and rear as well as head-on. (No, it's not fair to hold your breath.) Relax your muscles and be honest with yourself. Do you look reasonably proportioned or are you carrying excess baggage in the form of a protruding abdomen, saddlebag thighs and a bulging derriere? Are you pleased with the curves and muscles that you see or are you so thin that jutting hipbones, knees and ribs are your only visible protrusions?

Height and Weight Tables

What Should You Weigh?

Health experts stress the importance of maintaining "desirable body weight" through balancing energy intake with energy expenditure. The 1983 Metropolitan Height and Weight Tables are a widely recognized guide to the weights at which Americans are likely to live the longest.

The tables are based on mortality studies of more than 4 million insured people conducted by the Association of Life Insurance Medical Directors and the Society of Actuaries. These and other studies have consistently indicated that people whose weight was below the average for their height enjoyed the greatest longevity. In addition, a 1982 workshop sponsored by the Nutrition Coordinating Committee of the National Institutes of Health and the Centers for Disease Control agreed that overweight people tend to die sooner than average weight people, especially those who were overweight at a young age. On the other hand, people below average weight (although not far enough below to cause medical problems) tend to live longer.

The 1983 tables on page 40 are not labeled "desirable" or "ideal"; they simply indicate the weights at which studies show that people have the greatest longevity. Surprisingly, however, these weights are greater than when Metropolitan came out with its last set of such tables back in 1959. Yet the weights listed on the 1983 tables are still below the average weight of people in this country.

Note that the weights shown in the tables are a general guide for men and women aged 25–59. The tables provide a range of heights and body frames, since people come in a variety of sizes and shapes. There are also instructions on how to approximate your frame size by using the breadth of your elbows.

1983 Metropolitan Height and Weight Tables

Men					Women			
HEIGHT FT. IN.	SMALL FRAME	MEDIUM FRAME	LARGE FRAME		HEIGHT FT. IN.	SMALL FRAME	MEDIUM FRAME	LARGE FRAME
5 2	128–134	131–141	138–150		4 10	102–111	109–121	118–131
5 3	130–136	133–143	140–153		4 11	103–113	111–123	120–134
5 4	132–138	135–145	142–156		5 0	104–115	113–126	122–137
5 5	134–140	137–148	144–160		5 1	106–118	115–129	125–140
5 6	136–142	139–151	146–164		5 2	108–121	118–132	128–143
5 7	138–145	142–154	149–168		5 3	111–124	121–135	131–147
5 8	140–148	145–157	152–172		5 4	114–127	124–138	134–151
5 9	142–151	148–160	155–176		5 5	117–130	127–141	137–155
5 10	144–154	151–163	158–180		5 6	120–133	130–144	140–159
5 11	146–157	154–166	161–184		5 7	123–136	133–147	143–163
6 0	149–160	157–170	164–188		5 8	126–139	136–150	146–167
6 1	152–164	160–174	168–192		5 9	129–142	139–153	149–170
6 2	155–168	164–178	172–197		5 10	132–145	142–156	152–173
6 3	158–172	167–182	176–202		5 11	135–148	145–159	155–176
6 4	162–176	171–187	181–207		6 0	138–151	148–162	158–179

Weights at Ages 25–59 Based on Lowest Mortality. Weight in Pounds According to Frame (in indoor clothing weighing 5 lbs., shoes with 1″ heels).

Weights at Ages 25–59 Based on Lowest Mortality. Weight in Pounds According to Frame (in indoor clothing weighing 3 lbs., shoes with 1″ heels).

Source of basic data: *1979 Build Study*, Society of Actuaries and Association of Life Insurance Medical Directors of America, 1980.

How To Determine Your Body Frame By Elbow Breadth
To Make An Approximation Of Your Frame Size . . .

Extend your arm and bend the forearm upward at a 90 degree angle. Keep fingers straight and turn the inside of your wrist toward your body. If you have a caliper, use it to measure the space between the two prominent bones on either side of your elbow. Without a caliper, place thumb and index finger of your other hand on these two bones. Measure the space between your fingers against a ruler or tape measure. Compare it with these tables that list elbow measurements for medium framed men and women. Measurements lower than those listed indicate you have a small frame. Higher measurements indicate a large frame.

Men		Women	
Height in 1″ heels	Elbow Breadth	Height in 1″ heels	Elbow Breadth
5′2″–5′3″	2½″–2⅞″	4′10″–4′11″	2¼″–2½″
5′4″–5′7″	2⅝″–2⅞″	5′0″–5′3″	2¼″–2½″
5′8″–5′11″	2¾″–3″	5′4″–5′7″	2⅜″–2⅝″
6′0″–6′3″	2¾″–3⅛″	5′8″–5′11″	2⅜″–2⅝″
6′4″	2⅞″–3¼″	6′0″	2½″–2¾″

© 1983 Metropolitan Life Insurance Company

Also remember that the weights shown are for men and women wearing indoor clothing and shoes. It is assumed that male indoor clothing weighs five pounds and female indoor clothing weighs three pounds. A one-inch heel height was also assumed for both men and women. So, when weighing yourself nude, be sure to make the necessary adjustments for clothing and shoes.

An important consideration that is not taken into account on weight tables is how much of your weight is lean muscle and how much is fat. Because muscle weighs more than fat many well-conditioned athletes are considered *overweight* by height/weight charts—but certainly not overfat. Thus, muscle tone is also a consideration in determining your physique.

The Pinch Test

Most people under 50 have at least half of their body fat stored directly under the skin, so you can get a rough idea of how much fat you carry by having someone pinch your flesh, between their thumb and forefinger, on the back of your upper arm midway between your shoulder and elbow, while you are standing with your arm hanging at your side. The skin should be pulled away from the muscle so only the skin and fat are being held. If the distance between fingertips is more than one inch, you are probably overfat. If the pinch is less than ½-inch thick, you may be too thin.

The Belt-line Test (For Men)

Place a belt around your waist. Mark the spot where you fasten the ends. Now place the belt around your chest. If you are wider at the waist than at the chest, it's probably time to shed a few pounds.

If you want more exact information about your body composition, a doctor, dietitian or other health professional can precisely measure the amount of body fat you have with a device called a skinfold caliper. This information can then be used to determine your percentage of body fat. Body fat should account for about 15 percent in men and 19 percent in women. Generally, men with over 20–25 percent body fat and women with over 30 percent body fat are considered obese.

If you have decided that you are not currently at your desirable weight, the following formula can give you an approximate goal.

The Approximate Weight Rule (±10%)

Women: Allow 100 pounds for the first 5 feet in height, plus 5 pounds for each additional inch.

Men: Allow 106 pounds for the first 5 feet in height, plus 6 pounds for each additional inch.

Determining Your Calorie Needs

Your body needs a certain amount of energy every day to perform all of its functions. Food furnishes energy that is measured in units called calories. Calories keep your heart pumping, your lungs breathing, your body temperature just right and your muscles working. It's important to know how many calories your body needs for these functions, because any extra energy is stored as fat.

To determine the approximate number of calories your body needs to maintain its present weight, use the following simple formulas:

If you are not very active, multiply your current weight by 14.

If you are moderately active, multiply by 15.

If you are very active, multiply by 16.

If you are not quite sure which formula is right for you, refer to the table called "Determining Your Calorie Needs" on the next page. This table lists the calorie costs of various activities and exercises and can give you a more individual assessment of the calories you expend each day.

To use this chart, first keep a 24-hour diary of your activities on a typical day, being careful to record the length of time that you spend at each activity. Record your activities on a form like the table on the next page and multiply the time spent by calorie cost of each activity. The heavier you are, the greater the number of calories needed for the activity. Add up your total and you have an approximation of the calories you need to maintain your present weight.

Losing, Maintaining and Gaining

Regardless of whether you want to lose weight, gain weight or maintain your present weight, calories do count. And even if you fail to count them—your body never fails to do so.

Balancing your weight is all a matter of supply and demand. Consider the following facts:

If you eat fewer calories than your body needs for energy, you will lose weight. Your body will use its own stored fat to make up the deficit.

If you eat just enough calories to meet your body's energy needs, you will maintain your weight.

Determining Your Calorie Needs

Daily Activities	Calorie Expenditure Per Hour		Hours	Total Calories
	Women	Men		
Sleeping	54-66	60-72		
Very Light Activities: Sitting, Laboratory Work, Typing, Sewing, Ironing, Painting, Driving	up to 120	up to 150		
Light Activities: Carpentry, Washing Clothes, Shopping, Cooking, Washing Dishes, Electrical Work	132-234	150-294		
Moderate Activities: Gardening, Washing Floors, Vacuuming, Painting, Plastering	240-354	300-444		
Heavy Activities: Construction Work, Logging	360-600	450-720		
Sports and Exercise Walking (18-minute mile)	354	450		
Running 11-minute mile 8.5-minute mile 5-minute mile	576 750 1056	600 900 1200		
Swimming Pleasure (25 yards/ minute) Crawl (20-50 yards/ minute) Backstroke (20-40 yards/minute)	324 258-570 210-450	360 360-750 840		
Tennis	372	420-660		
Cross-Country Skiing	630	540-1020		
Downhill Skiing	516	480-720		
Bike Riding (5-15 mph)	270-576	300-720		
Handball or Squash	522	600		
	TOTAL		24 Hours	

If you eat more calories than your body needs for energy, you will gain weight. Your body will store the excess energy as body fat.

Each pound of fat your body stores represents 3,500 calories of unused energy. Few of us need 3,500 calories each day to meet our energy needs. That's why, despite the claims of miracle diets, it is almost impossible for anyone to lose a pound of fat every day, even if he or she eats absolutely nothing.

On the other hand, simply adding an 8-ounce glass of orange juice (120 calories) each day to your usual intake would add up to a weight gain of 12½ pounds in a year's time. While if you just cut out one tablespoon of oil (120 calories) from your daily diet, a year later you would weigh 12½ pounds less.

When you think about how much calories really do count, it may be hard to believe that anyone can maintain the same weight. But while the average person consumes between 800,000 and 900,000 calories each year, he or she expends more than 99 percent of them, maintaining a stable weight for years on end.

IV
Win at Losing

"Four out of five people who lose weight eventually regain it."

"Only 2 percent of those people who lose weight manage to keep it off."

"Almost all diets fail in the long run."

How many times have you heard these often quoted diet "facts"? Did you know they may not be facts at all? Strikingly different results were reported in a study published in the scientific journal *American Psychologist*.

The author was Dr. Stanley Schachter, a professor of psychology at Columbia University, and a leading authority on addictive behavior—addiction to drugs, addiction to smoking and addiction to food. He interviewed 83 of the 84 members of the Psychology Department of Columbia University as well as 78 of the 79 year-round merchants and tradespeople from a small town on Long Island, N.Y.

He discovered that of this total of 161 people, 46 had a history of obesity and 40 of these had tried to lose weight at some time. Of the 40 who had tried to lose weight, 57 percent of the women and 65 percent of the men had lost an average of 35 pounds and kept the weight off until the time of the study, an average of 10 years later.

What's the explanation for this seeming contradiction? First, before Dr. Schachter's study, statistics published about weight loss efforts were derived from the results of weight-loss therapy groups. These groups are usually composed of people who feel they cannot lose weight by themselves. Dr. Schachter's study looked at a group of people who were *not* a part of a weight-loss therapy group. Furthermore, Dr. Schachter found that 72 percent of the successful weight losers he interviewed had lost their extra pounds by themselves without outside help of any kind. The other 28 percent of those successful at weight loss had tried at some time to lose weight with the help of psychotherapy, physicians, hypnotists and weight-loss groups.

What does all this mean? The study shows that people can and do lose weight and keep it off. It also shows that the majority of those most successful seem to be people with the willpower to change their eating habits on a long-term basis without depending on outside help. Because the majority of these people don't join therapy groups, their successes do not become part of the usually reported data.

It's also important to remember that Dr. Schachter's positive findings are based on the results of a lifetime effort to control weight—a lifetime that may have involved one or many attempts to lose.

So don't give up because you haven't been successful at long-term weight loss before. Chances are that you learned something in those attempts—even if it was only learning that there is no quick and easy way to slim down.

Fattening eating habits are the result of years of conditioning. It takes time to recognize the bad habits and substitute more healthful ones that will, in the long run, lead toward a permanent solution to the weight problem. Lifelong weight control is not easy, but it can be, and has been done successfully. *You* can do it, too.

Overweight—But Why?

The "why" of a weight problem cannot be answered simply. The more scientists investigate the causes, the more complex they appear. But the basic fact remains: People gain weight whenever they take in more calories than they expend.

This fact, however, neither explains the cause of obesity, nor indicates the cure. Obesity results from a complex interaction of variables, not simply "overeating" per se. Heredity, environment, behavior, differences in metabolism, and activity level all play a role.

Genetics vs. Environment

There is little doubt that body size runs in families. Research shows that children with one obese parent have a 40 percent chance of becoming obese themselves. Children with two normal weight parents have a 93 percent chance of following in their footsteps. Is this phenomenon due to "nature" or "nurture"? The answer is probably some of each.

Early studies of the causes of obesity tend to emphasize "nature" or heredity. Scientists discovered that they could breed strains of obese mice. A classic 1930's study of human identical twins reared apart found striking similarities in their weights. But because so many other variables ultimately affect a person's weight, it is more likely that only a "tendency" to gain weight is inherited. The genetic tendency doesn't have to become reality.

Family food and fitness habits generally appear to exert a greater influence on a child's eventual weight than family genes. Recent studies show that the weights of adopted children are just as likely to resemble their adoptive parents' weights as those of natural children. Thus, nurture clearly seems to be involved. But, no one knows for sure.

Family Habits

The home environment is especially important in determining body weight. Quite simply, children learn the eating and exercise habits of their parents. Overeating at mealtime, indulging daily in rich desserts, excessive snacking and not exercising are habits often learned early that are difficult to break and usually carry over into adulthood.

Attitudes

Children also develop attitudes and feelings about food that can influence their future eating habits. For instance, some people are prompted by boredom, depression, loneliness and other emotions to stuff themselves with a particular food because it is associated with pleasant experiences in their childhood. Others may feel guilty at the sight of leftover food because of remembered parental admonishments to "clean your plate." Such emotions and attitudes can strongly affect the way an individual uses or abuses food.

Too Many Fat Cells

Eating habits formed early in life are hard to change, and fat gained at a young age is hard to lose. According to the popular "fat cell" theory, overweight babies and chubby preteens develop more fat storage cells than normal weight babies and preteens. Apparently, fat cells develop rapidly during periods of growth—before birth, in infancy and in early and preadolescence. Once developed, these fat cells never go away. Dieting can shrink their size, but not their number. According to the theory, they always remain in the body waiting to be "filled up" at the slightest increase in calories. A person who is overweight at these critical periods of growth may be more likely to face a lifetime struggle with a tendency to gain weight.

But don't think you are safe from excessive fat cells just because you are past adolescence. Recent evidence suggests that extra fat cells can be added any time there is a rapid weight gain. Pregnancy, for instance, is a high risk period for fat cell increase. Thus, excessive weight gain during pregnancy can lead to a subsequent weight problem. Pregnant women should follow their doctor's advice regarding what constitutes an adequate weight gain.

Changing Times

These variables and theories help explain individual weight problems, but you might still be wondering how *so many* Americans (80 million) got too fat.

For one thing, our lifestyles have changed drastically since the beginning of the industrial revolution. American society evolved from rural and agrarian to highly technological and urban, and that change affected its people. We are more sedentary than our predecessors. Today's children ride to school rather than walk, and most spend hours sitting in front of the television set. As adults, we drive or ride everywhere and rely on a variety of labor-saving devices to do our house and yard work. To top it all off, most of us have sedentary jobs for eight or more hours a day.

Our food supply is more abundant today, too. Rich desserts, bakery goods, sauces, dressings—just about any food you want is in the supermarket, usually requiring only a minimum amount of effort to prepare. We eat one-third of our meals away from home. Abundant food is an accepted—in fact, expected—part of home entertaining. Even recreational activities are surrounded by food. Who can go to a baseball game without buying a frankfurter, a soft drink or a beer? So although we no longer burn anywhere near as many calories as our predecessors, we are constantly tempted to eat more. Eating more food and burning less energy in activity is exactly the right combination for gaining weight.

To get back on the right track those of us who are overweight need to readjust our habits by eating less and exercising more. But be sure to check with your doctor *before* you begin any diet or exercise program.

Facing the Facts About Losing Fat

Americans spend billions of dollars on weight-reducing regimens every year, and many are tempted by the ones that hinge on a miracle ingredient or an outlandish scheme. These dieters are not only wasting their money, but may also be risking their health.

Beware of the Fakes

In most health professions, education standards are controlled by licensing laws that protect the public. But in nutrition, anyone can declare himself or herself an "expert." While many people who label themselves "nutritionist" hold legitimate health credentials, others have mail-order B.S., M.S. and Ph.D. degrees from unaccredited correspondence schools, $50 "professional nutritionist" or "nutritional consultant" certificates from impressive-sounding credential mills, degrees in an area unrelated to nutrition, or nothing at all.

Under the "freedom of speech" protection of the Constitution, these self-styled "nutritionists" can make any claims they wish regarding nutrition. Many of them have private practices for "nutrition consultations," where some utilize useless tests such as hair analysis to convince their clients to follow unusual diet regimes with no proven merit, or to take the megavitamins, minerals, herbs and "organic" foods that they sell. Others may author books about nutrition that are not based on scientific facts. All too often, these become best sellers because the authors appear on radio and television shows and are quoted in newspapers and magazines. Their advice usually is a mixture of some facts, but also many half-truths and outright nonsense.

Getting Reliable Advice

Before starting any new diet regimen, including a weight reduction plan, consult your physician. If your doctor is unable to answer your questions, he or she can protect you from the nutrition quack by referring you to a qualified professional nutrition counselor.

If you want nutrition information or help with your diet, you may want to consult a registered dietitian (R.D.). These professionals must hold a four-year degree in a dietetic program approved by the American Dietetic Association (ADA), have completed an approved dietetic internship or the equivalent, have passed a nationally administered registration examination, and must maintain proficiency through continuing education that has also been approved by the ADA. Registered dietitians can be found in hospital nutrition departments, university food and nutrition departments, public health facilities, industry and private practice.

Miracle Diets and Magic Pills

A basic understanding of nutrition can help you protect yourself from any fad diet that could be harmful. (For information on where you can write to in order to learn more about nutrition, see the Appendix.) Let's look at the extravagant claims and unscientific reasoning of some types of popular diets and the health risks associated with each.

Claim: Fasting is an excellent way to lose weight because it also rids the body of toxic wastes and gives the vital organs a rest.

Fact: Fasting does produce rapid weight loss, but you're not losing the weight you should be losing. Instead of just getting rid of unwanted fat, you also lose protein from the muscles and vital organs, body water, vitamins and minerals. Fasting has not been shown to contribute any benefits to overall health. On a fast you may experience wrenching hunger pangs, weakness, dizziness and headache, all to lose a few pounds that will probably creep right back on once you start eating normally again. And you are placing your body under severe physical stress, which could lead to serious medical problems.

   The body removes toxic wastes more effectively by the normal bowel movements that result from regular meals than by the erratic bowel movements that accompany fasting. Fasting rests no vital organs.

Claim: Very low-calorie formula diets are safe when they contain the Recommended Daily Allowances of vitamins and minerals plus enough protein to prevent muscle loss.

Fact: Anyone on a diet of 600 calories or less per day will start losing lean body mass (muscle) from day one. An unpredictable amount of this lost muscle can be from the heart. A number of people who died while on the popular liquid protein diets were found to have a loss of heart muscle (cardiac atrophy) at their death. Any diet containing less than 800 calories per day should be followed only under the strict supervision of a physician.

Claim: Certain foods such as cakes, pies, white bread and potato chips, although they have the same number of calories as other foods, are more likely to put weight on you.

Fact: A calorie is a calorie is a calorie. Five hundred calories of bread will not make you one ounce fatter than 500 calories of tuna fish. Eating more calories than you burn up in activity makes you gain weight regardless of the source of the calories.

Claim: A low-carbohydrate diet is the quickest way to lose weight because it forces your body to metabolize your stored fat and burn it off at an accelerated rate.

Fact: Low-carbohydrate diets are often popular for weight loss because a very low-carbohydrate intake causes the body to lose abnormally large amounts of water. This loss of water shows up on the scales as a loss of weight, which most dieters mistakenly interpret as a loss of body fat. Unfortunately, replacing the water means replacing the weight. Taking in fewer calories than you need will cause your body to draw on its stored fat reserves for energy, but restricting carbohydrates will not make you burn the stored fat faster or more efficiently than restricting calories from any other food source.

There are potential health hazards with a low-carbohydrate diet, too. When the body has a limited supply of carbohydrate and must burn fat for energy, chemical residue called ketones are left behind. Up to a point, ketones can be recycled for energy, but beyond that, they build up in the blood stream, causing the dieter to feel weak, nauseated and generally miserable.

Claim: Eating a high-protein diet can help you lose weight because it takes more calories to digest protein than to digest other nutrients.

Fact: Although there may be slight differences in the number of calories used during the digestion of protein, fat and carbohydrate, these differences are insignificant in a balanced diet consisting of foods from the Basic Four.

One of the problems with high-protein diets is that most foods considered to be "protein food" also contain significant amounts of fat, which has more calories per gram than protein or carbohydrate. For instance, a T-bone steak contains about 80 percent of its calories as fat. Many high-protein diets are in reality high-fat, high-cholesterol, high-calorie regimens, as well as high protein.

Claim: Grapefruit and certain other fruits contain enzymes that burn up fat.

Fact: This is simply untrue. There are no magic fat-burning foods, enzymes, pills or other substances. All foods have calories. Half of a grapefruit contains about 50 calories, so if you ate one before every meal you would add 16 pounds in one year's time. And, just for the record, any enzymes from pills or foods that are taken by mouth are broken down into their component amino acids by digestion in the stomach and small intestine. They are not absorbed intact and therefore cannot function as enzymes within the body.

Claim: Spirulina works as a natural appetite suppressant because it contains the amino acid phenylalanine, which acts on the brain's appetite center.

Fact: Spirulina is a type of algae that grows in stagnant ponds. It does contain phenylalanine in its protein (as do all other protein-containing foods), but there is no reliable scientific evidence that phenylalanine in protein, or alone, is effective as an appetite suppressant in any way. There is a similar lack of evidence to back up claims that spirulina promotes muscle growth or "quick energy" for athletes.

Claim: High-fiber diets and high-fiber supplements or bulking agents such as glucomannan are weight loss aids because they help transport food through the digestive system faster, causing many calories to pass out of the body before they are digested.

Fact: Fiber does not cause food to be transported through the intestinal tract at a rate so fast that calories cannot be absorbed. If this occurred, such supplements would also cause bloating, stomach distress and diarrhea. Including a moderate amount of bulky, fiber-containing food (fruits and vegetables, whole grain breads and cereals) in your diet is a smart move during weight loss—or at any other time—because they are nutritious and filling, yet relatively low in calories.

Claim: If you take diet pills, you can safely lose weight without cutting calories.

Fact: Diet pills do not take weight off by themselves. You must still restrict your calorie intake or you won't lose an ounce. Some diet pills may suppress the appetite to some extent at first, but their effectiveness wears off over several weeks as the body builds up a tolerance to them.

But the effects of most diet pills on your appetite may be less important than what they do to your health. Most nonprescription pills contain phenylpropanolamine (PPA) and can cause undesirable side effects such as headache, blurred vision, rapid pulse, nervousness, insomnia, dizziness, heart palpitations and increased blood pressure. Phenylpropanolamine is known to be unsafe for pregnant women and people with certain medical problems. Prescription diet pills are usually amphetamines, which can be addicting and extremely dangerous.

Claim: "Cellulite" is not ordinary fat, but a combination of fat, toxic wastes and water that can be removed only through special exercises and a special diet.

Fact: The term "cellulite" is often used to describe the dimpled fat deposits found on the hips and thighs of many women. But according to the American Medical Association, "there is no medical condition known or described as cellulite in this country." The truth is that "cellulite" is just plain fat, and the only effective means of removal is weight loss by reducing caloric intake and/or increasing exercise. No "toxic wastes" have ever been demonstrated in these fat deposits by anyone.

Sensible Alternatives

What type of diet plan *will* allow you to lose weight without endangering your health? Here are five questions you can use to evaluate any weight loss diet.

Does the diet include a variety of foods from each of the Basic Four Food Groups? A diet that leaves out any group of foods is not nutritionally balanced, and any diet that is out of balance, regardless of which food group or nutrient it favors, can be dangerous. A wide range and balance of nutrients are found naturally in the Four Food Groups in absorbable forms.

Are there fewer calories in the weight-loss diet than in the diet you normally eat? Remember you can only lose weight by reducing your caloric intake below your energy output. There is no special combination of foods or nutrients that allows you to lose weight without cutting calories. Diets that let you eat "all you want of x, y and z" may only work because the monotony of eating the same foods daily dulls your appetite, causing you to eat less food and fewer calories.

Does the diet depend on any pills, powders or other gimmicks to be effective? There are no magic diet aids that promote quick, easy and safe weight loss. If you lose weight on a diet plan that requires the purchase of a special product, it is because you are reducing your calorie intake. The "miracle" reducing aid simply assures the promoter of making big bucks—at your expense.

Diets that depend on special canned or powdered formulas to replace one or more meals are usually unbalanced and, like all "monotony" diets, they are hard to stick with and teach nothing about how to keep weight off. All of these formulas are an expensive source of the same nutrients easily obtainable from common foods.

Does the diet promise quick, drastic weight losses such as "lose 20 pounds in two weeks"? To lose a pound of stored fat, the body must burn 3,500 calories more than it takes in. Few people could burn this amount of energy in a day even if they ate nothing. A crash diet may cause the scale to plummet at first, but rapid, early weight loss results from loss of body water and the scale inevitably creeps upward again as soon as you begin eating normally. A weight loss of 1 to 2 pounds per week is a reasonable goal. A weight loss of 4 pounds or more a week is unsafe if not under the close supervision of a competent health professional.

Is the diet made up of a variety of foods that you enjoy and that is easily available to you? If the diet plan is not something you can stick with without becoming bored and frustrated, any weight you lose on it isn't likely to stay off for long. Long-term success demands a diet plan that fits your lifestyle as well as your budget and is flexible enough to include your favorite foods—in moderation.

Losing Weight—The Fitness Equation

Once you accept the fact that no diet will melt away excess pounds without smaller portions and other modifications in your eating habits, you're ready for *Eat Well, Be Well's* healthful, workable and delicious approach to long-term weight loss success.

The formula for losing weight is quite *simple:*

Less Food + More Activity = Weight Loss. How much weight you lose depends upon the factors on the left side of the equation.

Let's take an example. Say you want to lose one pound each week (1 pound = 3,500 calories) and you have calculated your caloric needs to be 2,000 calories per day. If you eat 500 calories a day less than your daily caloric output without changing your activity level, you'll lose one pound by the end of each week.

Equation I:

Less Food (Calories)		More Activity (Calories)		Weight (Calories)
(500 × 7 days)	+	0	=	3,500 calories or one pound weight loss

Recall, that the weight loss discussed here is fat loss. During the first week or two on a diet, you will probably lose some water along with the fat, so part of the weight loss is water loss.

If you add exercise every day, that pound will come off with a reduction of fewer food calories. For instance, jogging daily for 25 minutes or walking briskly for 40 minutes burns up an extra 250 calories, so you can lose one pound each week by cutting only 250 calories from your usual diet. That still leaves you 1,750 calories of food to enjoy! Just follow Equation II.

Equation II:

Less Food (Calories)		More Activity (Calories)		Weight (Calories)
(250 × 7 days)	+	(250 × 7 days)	=	3,500 calories or one pound weight loss

If you reduce your food intake by 500 calories (to 1,500 calories per day) *plus* exercise for 25–30 minutes, you can lose 1½ pounds each week. It's as simple as the next equation.

Equation III:

Less Food (Calories)		More Activity (Calories)		Weight (Calories)
(500 × 7 days)	+	(250 × 7 days)	=	5,250 calories or 1½ pounds weight loss

Although it is possible to lose weight just by lowering food intake and making no change in activity, most people find it easier to reduce by a combination of increasing physical activity and cutting calories. Not only does increased activity make it possible to lose weight without a severe calorie reduction, but regular exercise is also important for good muscle tone, general good health and a sense of well-being.

Basic Types of Exercises

Regular moderate exercise can improve your physical *and* mental well-being. Helping your body burn up unnecessary fat, firming up muscles, and flattening bulges are only a few of the benefits you can expect.*

*Remember to check with your doctor before beginning any exercise program.

There are three basic types of exercises: stretching, calisthenics and aerobics. The type of exercise you choose can make a big difference in the results you get.

Stretching

Stretching exercises are recommended before and after any strenuous sport or activity. For the most benefit, you want to try to stretch as many joints of your body as possible—your neck, shoulders, hips, back and ankles. Stretches are done slowly and smoothly, without jerking or bouncing. That will limber and relax your muscles so they don't become short and tight, and keep joints flexible.

For instance, to stretch the back of your legs and spine, try this: in a standing position with knees slightly bent, slowly lean over to touch your toes, keeping your arms extended, head and neck relaxed. Reach as far as you can, without bouncing, and hold that position for about 15 seconds, then come back up gradually.

Stretching exercises like this one relieve muscle tension and provide a sense of overall relaxation. But don't count on stretching to burn extra calories.

Many people confuse stretching exercises with warming up, but they are not the same. Stretching does not raise muscle temperature, so stretching exercises should *follow* your warm-up activity, not begin your exercise session. Trying to stretch cold muscles can lead to injury.

Calisthenics

Sit-ups, leg-lifts and "the bicycle" are good examples of calisthenics. These shape-up exercises will tone and firm under-used muscles. But like stretching, calisthenics won't burn many extra calories or help you lose weight, unless you do an intensive series of them for 20 to 30 minutes at a time.

Aerobics

Aerobic exercises use the body's large muscles in continuous, sustained and rhythmical movement. The best ones include:

Brisk walking	Roller skating
Jogging or running	Aerobic dancing
Swimming	Disco dancing
Riding a stationary bike	Jumping rope
Outdoor bike-riding	Cross-country skiing
Ice skating	

Note that sports like tennis or baseball are not on this list. That's because in order for aerobics to benefit your body, you must get a vigorous, *continuous* workout for at least 20 minutes. Tennis (except for singles) and baseball involve lots of stand-still time, waiting for the ball. For aerobic conditioning and maximum calorie expenditure, choose an activity that keeps you steadily moving.

Aerobic Advantages

Aerobics are loaded with benefits. If done regularly, these activities help improve many body functions. They strengthen the heart, improve circulation, aid in digestion and elimination, build some muscle endurance and even help you sleep. A good aerobic workout also increases your metabolic rate so your body burns more calories and fat. You may want to refer to the table on page 43 to learn how many calories you can expend in various sports and activities.

Your Heart Rate

In order to get the most benefit from your aerobic program, you must raise your heart rate and keep it up for at least 20 to 30 minutes. In exercise science terminology, this increase is called your "training heart rate." It should be 60 to 85 percent of your maximum heart rate if you are basically healthy.

To monitor your heart rate while performing an aerobic activity, simply place your fingertips lightly on the palm side of the wrist near the thumb, on the large arteries on either side of your neck, or place your hand over your heart. Count the number of beats for 10 seconds and multiply that figure by six—that's your heart rate for one minute. Check the table on the next page for the approximate training heart rate appropriate for your age and sex. If you are not within your recommended range and feel good after your exercise, you may want to pick up your pace. You probably are not working hard enough to get the full benefits of your aerobic activity.

But remember that the numbers on the chart are given only to provide you with an *idea* of your training heart rate. Don't become so concerned with "average" values that you forget to listen to your body. People vary. Never push yourself to the point of shortness of breath, pain or dizziness.

Pace Yourself

When just beginning an aerobic program, you'll probably reach your training heart rate fairly quickly. To avoid overdoing it, check with your doctor *before* you start, so you can plan an exercise

Your Training Heart Rate

WOMEN

Age	Minimum	Optimum	Maximum
25	130	157	185
30	126	153	180
35	123	149	175
40	119	145	170
45	116	140	165
50	112	136	160
55	109	132	155
60	105	128	150
65	102	123	145

MEN

Age	Minimum	Optimum	Maximum
25	137	166	195
30	133	162	190
35	130	157	185
40	128	153	180
45	123	149	175
50	119	145	170
55	116	140	165
60	112	136	160
65	109	132	155

Source: Gabe Mirkin, "Fitnotes," in *The Jogger*, 1981

schedule that's right for you. Many people have hidden heart problems, and seeing a doctor for an evaluation is an essential precaution.

Begin any aerobic activity slowly to warm up your muscles and then do your stretching exercises. Your warm-up and stretching should take at least 10 minutes. Start out the first day of your program by doing your exercise for about 8 to 10 minutes, or less if you begin to feel tired. After a week or 10 days, increase your session by about 5 minutes. Do the same until you reach your fitness goal. And keep it up.

When you're exercising at the right pace, you'll be breathing deeply, but you shouldn't be panting or gasping for breath. A good rule is—if you can't carry on a conversation while you're exercising, you're pushing too hard.

The key to increased fitness through exercise is *regularity* and *progression*, that is, doing more next month than you are doing now, and even more six months later, and so on. Once you are "in shape" you'll need to spend at least 20 to 30 minutes, three times a week for cardiovascular fitness, and you may want to exercise four to five times a week to burn up extra calories and fat. And, the more active you are, the more freedom you can have with your diet.

The Calorie Burners

No one is perfect; sooner or later most of us will cheat on our diets. Maybe it will be a favorite chocolate cake on a birthday, or a special dinner party at a gourmet restaurant. Situations are going to arise when you just can't help but go over your calorie limit. Do not despair. Balance means going extra easy on what you eat the next day, and increasing your activity level a bit. Take a look at the calories you can burn with just a little effort:

A Lunch Time Splurge—What Do You Do?

Hamburger (3 ounces)		250 calories
French fries, regular		220 calories
Vanilla shake		350 calories
	Total	820 calories

Exercise Remedies:

Go home and scrub floors. Vacuuming, sweeping and mopping for one hour will burn up that vanilla shake (370 exercise calories).

Jog for 30 minutes—you'll lose 300 calories, the burger.

Put on your favorite music and dance for 40 minutes and the French fries will be long gone. (You'll burn about 300 calories.)

A Few Weaknesses

Chocolate ice cream cone	165 calories
Chocolate nougat candy bar	250 calories
Chocolate-chip cookies (3 medium)	150 calories

In Case You Indulge:

Work out for 30 minutes on the tennis court. Play singles and *run* for the shots. You will burn up about 270 calories—no more candy bar.

Swim laps for 20 minutes. You'll use 180 calories in the process and leave the ice cream cone behind.

Get outside. One-half hour of gardening will get rid of the chocolate chip cookies. You'll burn about 160 calories.

The trick is to keep busy and active. You won't be around food when you exercise, and you burn up all those calories at the same time.

Don't Just Sit There—Get Up and Move

If you are trying to control your weight, you should try to exercise as often as you can *throughout* the day—especially if you have a desk job. Remember, every little bit of exercise will help you burn extra calories. Here are some helpful tips:

Take the stairs whenever possible; avoid elevators and escalators.

Park your car at some distance from your destination and walk. Or get off the bus or subway a few stops earlier.

Walk whenever possible; don't take the car or public transportation for distances under ½ mile. And walk briskly, pulling in your stomach and firming your buttocks.

Instead of sitting in front of the television, lie on the floor and exercise.

Carry your own groceries and pick up your own dry cleaning, rather than having them delivered.

Follow the principles of balance, variety and moderation in your diet and moderation, regularity and progression in your exercise programs for lasting rewards in your health and well-being. When you're eating properly and exercising regularly, you'll look better and feel better about yourself.

Planning Your Personal Diet Strategy

When you are watching your caloric intake, it's more important than ever to eat a variety of foods every day. You can't afford foods that don't pay their way in the nutrients your body needs. But you can be sure you are getting your quota of vitamins and minerals and keep your calories in check if you follow the guidelines of the Basic Four.

4 servings from the Vegetable/Fruit Group
4 servings from the Bread/Cereal Group
2 servings from the Milk/Cheese Group
2 servings from the Meat/Poultry/Fish/Bean Group

This may seem to be a lot of food. But if you follow the *recommended servings sizes*, you'll average about 1,200 calories each day—a reasonable, nutritionally sound goal for weight loss. For a quick review of the Basic Four Food Groups and recommended serving sizes see pages 12–13. If you figured your daily weight-loss diet calories to be much below 1,200—the necessary level for meeting all your nutrient needs—consider increasing your activity to burn the extra calories or settle for losing weight at a slower rate. If your daily diet level calories are more than you need to meet the Basic Four recommendations, you can choose higher calorie selections within each group (low-fat milk instead of skim milk, for instance), have more than the recommended number of servings from some groups (such as 6 servings from the Bread/Cereal Group instead of 4), have larger portion sizes than recommended (4 ounces of chicken, perhaps, instead of 3 ounces), or include a few foods from the "extra" food group (sweets, fats and alcohol).

That's the basic plan. Now, the first step to creating a balanced diet that will meet your personal needs is to take a look at what you are eating now to pinpoint any problem areas. Begin by writing down everything you eat and drink on a typical day. Don't forget to record the amounts, too.

First, check how many servings you had from each of the food groups and add up the totals. How close to the recommended number of servings did you come? Shortchanging one or more of the Basic Four Food Groups on a regular basis will inevitably lead to skipping some essential nutrients. Your first goal, therefore, should be to eat more foods from any group that is lacking in your diet. On the other hand, if you have an abundance of servings from one group, you may need to do some substituting or cutting back.

Next, if you want to find out how many calories are in the foods you ate, consult a book that provides this information. You may purchase two such publications from USDA: *USDA Pocket Guide— Calories and Weight* for $2.25, and *Nutritive Value of Foods* for $2.75. Both may be ordered from the Superintendent of Documents, U.S. Government Printing Office, Washington, DC, 20402.

This is time-consuming and not essential, but you will find it helpful to be familiar with the number of calories in the foods that you eat often. You may even find some surprises that will help explain your weight problem.

Take the case of Susan. She's 35 and a working mother, always pressed for time. As you can see from the chart showing her sample day's diet on page 64, Susan grabs breakfast from the pastry cart at the office and lunches quickly each weekday at a nearby fast-food restaurant. Then, at dinnertime, tired from a long day at work, she has little desire to spend a lot of time in the kitchen.

Susan would like to eat better nutritionally and lose some weight, but she feels this is beyond her control. And she refuses to give up certain foods she enjoys, such as her nightly glass of wine with dinner. But though Susan sees changing her bad habits as too difficult to accomplish, in reality, she can cut calories and add nutrition with a minimum of effort.

On the chart you can see that Susan came up short in the Milk/ Cheese Group, so we balanced her new modified diet by adding cheese at breakfast, sprinkling parmesan cheese on her noodles at dinner, and substituting nutrient-dense skim milk for her usual snack of high-calorie ice cream.

Now let's see where she can eliminate excess calories. A good place to start is by cutting out the "extras" from the Fats/Sweets/Alcohol Group. The foods provide palatability and calories, but few nutri-ents. You don't have to give up all these foods, provided you are meeting your Basic Four requirements. But, there are sure to be some items you can easily live without. Susan didn't want to give up her wine with dinner, but she was willing to forego the cola, tartar sauce, and the butter on noodles as well as use only half as much sugar in her coffee.

Different foods within each group contain varying amounts of calo-ries, and cooking methods can also make big differences. So, check the "Best Bets for Waist Watchers" on pages 15–18. These selec-tions give good return in valuable nutrients for every calorie they contain. Susan streamlined her calories without cutting out nutri-ents by selecting a slice of whole wheat bread instead of breakfast pastry, substituting an apple for apple pie and a salad for French fries at lunch, and by choosing to have broiled fish instead of breaded fish sticks for dinner.

Another simple adjustment that helps many people lose problem pounds is reducing the size of portions. Most of us tend to overload our plates, especially with meat (8 or 10 ounces of steak, for exam-ple, when 3 ounces is the recommended portion size). Even a healthful diet balanced according to the Basic Four can be fatten-ing if you eat too much of any food. Susan trimmed down her portions of orange juice and noodles to the recommended ½ cup; switched the "quarter pound" burger for the regular size, and cut her serving of fish at dinner to a moderate 3 ounces.

Susan's new calorie-trimmed sample day diet on page 65 supplied all of the recommended servings for the Basic Four and still had room for more—an extra snack (raisins), another vegetable (broc-coli), graham crackers, a teaspoon of margarine and a glass of wine—all for about 1,200 calories. That's more than 1,000 calories less than her original day's intake!

Susan's Unmodified Sample Day Diet

	Calories	Vegetable/Fruit Group	Bread/Cereal Group	Milk/Cheese Group	Meat/Poultry/Fish/Bean Group	"Extra" Group Fats/Sweets/Alcohol
Breakfast						
Pastry (1 large)	275		1			
Orange juice (1 cup)	120	2				
Coffee (1 cup)	2					
Sugar (2 tsp.)	30					1
Lunch						
Quarter pound burger					1	
with bun	424		2			
French fries (1 serving)	220	1				
Cola (12 ounces)	144					1
Apple pie	253	1				
Dinner						
Breaded fish sticks (5 ounces)	250				2	
Tartar sauce (1 tbsp.)	75					1
Noodles (¾ cup)	150		1½			
with butter (2 tsp.)	66					1
Parslied carrots (½ cup)	25	1				
White wine (1 glass)	90					1
Snack						
Ice cream (½ cup)	135			⅓		
Totals	2259	5	4½	⅓	3	5

Modification of
Susan's Sample Day Diet

	Calories	Vegetable/Fruit Group	Bread/Cereal Group	Milk/Cheese Group	Meat/Poultry/Fish/Bean Group	"Extra" Group Fats/Sweets/Alcohol
Breakfast						
Cheddar cheese (1 ounce)	113			¾		
Whole-wheat bread (1 slice)	65		1			
Orange juice (½ cup)	60	1				
Coffee (1 cup)	2					
Sugar (1 tsp.)	15					1
Lunch						
Hamburger (regular)					1	
with bun	255		2			
Tossed salad (1 cup)	20	1				
with lemon wedge	2					
Club soda (12 ounces)	0					
Apple	87	1				
Snack						
Raisins (2 tbsp.)	52	½				
Dinner						
Broiled fish (3 oz. cooked)	100				1	
with margarine (1 tsp.)	33					1
Noodles (½ cup)	100		1			
with Parmesan cheese						
(1 tbsp.)	21			¼		
Steamed broccoli (½ cup)	20	1				
Parslied carrots (½ cup)	25	1				
White wine (1 glass)	90					1
Snack						
Skim milk (1 cup)	90			1		
Graham crackers (2						
squares)	55		1			
Totals	1205	5½	5	2	2	3

The Basic Four can serve as a master plan to help anyone develop a realistic lifelong diet. Because you do the planning, you can be sure that the diet consists of foods that you like, that are easily available, and that are within your budget.

At first it may seem as if you have to spend a lot of time planning your meals and counting calories, but it will get easier, and your new eating pattern will quickly become a habit. The *Eat Well, Be Well®* recipes and meal plans will prove that watching calories need not take away the fun of cooking or eating.

The Dieter's Guide to Calorie Cutting

Were you surprised to find out how many calories were in your sample day's intake? It's easy to pick up extra calories without thinking, but it's also easy to eliminate excess calories if you learn to play the substitution game and find low-calorie stand-ins for many of the high-calorie foods in your diet.

Here are some slimming tips to start you on your way:

Cutting Fat Calories

Fat is the most compact form of calories in the diet, so becoming more fat conscious is the first step toward a slimmer you.

Rely on nonstick cookware and nonstick vegetable cooking sprays to prevent sticking, instead of oil or shortening.

Sauté foods such as onions, mushrooms, celery and garlic in bouillon, chicken stock, wine or seasoned water instead of in butter, margarine or oil.

Eat broth-based soups instead of cream soups, or make your own "cream" soups using yogurt, skim milk or vegetable purees. (See our Cream of Carrot Soup on page 100.)

Cook soups and stews ahead when using butter, margarine or shortening. Then refrigerate to allow the fat to rise to the top and harden; remove and discard the fat layer and reheat the food.

Never brown vegetables at the same time you brown meat. Vegetables are notorious fat sponges.

Have mustard on your sandwich instead of mayonnaise and save almost 30 calories per tablespoon.

Allow butter or margarine to soften before you put it on your roll or toast so it can be spread thinly—just enough for flavor.

Make your own diet butter or margarine by adding equal amounts of cold water and whip at high speed in blender or food processor.

Don't add butter or margarine to rice. Instead, add herbs and cook in a flavored broth or tomato juice to add almost calorie-free flavor.

It's not necessary to add oil to the water when cooking pasta; just stir it occasionally as it is cooking and the pasta will not stick together. When ready to serve, add just enough sauce to prevent sticking and serve additional sauce on the side.

Don't make the mistake of believing that nondairy creamers and nondairy toppings are low-fat or low-calorie. They are usually neither.

Try substituting evaporated skim milk in recipes that call for cream. Well-chilled evaporated skim milk can even be whipped. For best results, start with a chilled mixing bowl and chilled beaters.

Avoid prebasted turkeys. They are often injected with saturated coconut oil.

Save money while saving calories by substituting ground turkey in recipes that call for ground beef. Just be sure to cook the turkey well and add a little vegetable oil if necessary to compensate for the lack of fat.

It's not necessary to add fat to the skillet when browning most cuts of beef. If you put the meat into a cold skillet and heat slowly, the meat will release its own fat. Drain well before serving.

Have meatless entrees several times a week, but avoid recipes with excessive cheese, nuts, oils or creams. Some meatless dishes, such as quiche, have more fat than meat.

If you love mashed potatoes, whip them with skim milk, chicken broth, plain yogurt or low-fat buttermilk instead of the usual butter and whole milk.

Most salad dressings and dips are loaded with fat calories. Make your own, using plain low-fat yogurt, or cottage cheese that you have whipped in the blender. (See our Mexican Dip, page 89.)

Plain low-fat yogurt mixed with a touch of honey makes a wonderful low-fat dressing for a fruit dessert.

Skim milk, plain low-fat yogurt or low-fat buttermilk can be an excellent base for a delicious, nutritious beverage. Blend these dairy products with fresh or unsweetened frozen fruits and a little sweetener, if desired. If you want a milk shake, add cracked ice and blend.

Watch out for the hidden fat calories in many processed foods. Read labels carefully. (See page 195.)

Cutting Sugar Calories

Eating less sugar is another excellent way to cut down on calories because it doesn't cut out any nutrients. Here's how:

Begin to cut down on the amount of sugar you add to your food and beverages. This means cutting back on all kinds of sugar including honey, brown sugar, syrups and molasses. By cutting back slowly, your taste buds will adjust to the less sweet taste.

When fresh fruits aren't available, turn to fruits canned in natural juices or to unsweetened frozen fruits. Remember that dried fruits are proportionally higher in calories than fresh fruits because they contain less water.

For a gelatin salad or dessert, begin with unflavored gelatin and flavor it with fruit juices and unsweetened fruit—fresh, frozen or canned. (See Cranberry Citrus Waldorf Mold, page 107.)

Try fresh fruit purees instead of syrups for French toast and pancakes. If it is not quite sweet enough for you, add a little orange or apple juice concentrate.

Freeze seedless grapes or banana chunks for refreshing treats.

Skip the sugar often called for in tomato-based recipes. A grated carrot added to the sauce will provide natural low-calorie sweetness with a vitamin A bonus.

Check out the low-sugar jams, jellies and preserves in your supermarket.

If you have overripe fruits like peaches, nectarines or berries, puree and freeze to use as sauces later. Overripe is naturally sweet.

Make your own fresh fruit desserts with grapes, tangerine sections, diced apples and pears, a sliced banana and a dash of orange juice concentrate. One-half cup is about 70 calories.

Experiment with cutting down on sugar in cookies, cakes and quick breads. The sugar can often be reduced by one-third to one-half without loss of flavor.

Heighten the effect of sweetness in low-sugar desserts by adding sweet spices such as vanilla, ginger, nutmeg and cinnamon and go easy on sour or bitter ingredients such as lemon.

A 12-ounce can of most sweetened carbonated beverages contains 10 to 12 teaspoons of sugar. Make your own soda by mixing naturally sweet fruit juices, such as orange, grape, apple or pineapple with seltzer water or club soda.

Be aware that many processed foods have added sugar and, therefore, have more calories than you might think. Read labels. (See pages 194–195.)

Cutting Alcohol Calories

Alcohol consumption doesn't have to be an all or nothing proposition. Remember, it's up to you to decide how to spend any extra calories you have in your day's quota. To trim alcohol calories, try these hints:

Don't drink when you are hungry. You'll be more likely to drink too fast.

Be aware that alcohol is an appetite stimulant and can sabotage your willpower.

Alcohol has a dehydrating effect on the body, so if you feel thirsty while drinking, have a glass of water instead of another drink.

Lower the concentration of alcohol in your diet by diluting it with lots of water or club soda.

"Light" beers and wines contain fewer calories than standard beers and wines, but they still provide generous amounts if you don't practice moderation.

Avoid sweet liqueurs and cordials. They contain sweeteners, which add even more calories.

Try club soda or seltzer water with a splash of wine and a twist of lemon.

Leave all the alcohol calories behind by having plain tomato juice with the same seasonings you would use in a Bloody Mary.

Look for drink recipes such as our Hot Mulled Wine (page 190) that include nutritious ingredients to dilute the alcohol.

Psyching Up for Slimming Down

There's more to successful weight loss than getting your kitchen ready with the right foods. You also have to recognize and modify all of the attitudes and behaviors that have contributed to the problem in the first place.

A good way to start is by keeping a detailed record of your eating habits for at least a week. Write down what, when and where you eat, who you're eating with, what you're doing while you eat, and your mood or feelings at the time. If you are diligent in your record-keeping, you should be able to pinpoint *why* you tend to overeat, which situations or moods affect *what* and *how much* you eat, and how certain foods make you *feel*. You'll begin to understand the positive and negative "cues" that influence your eating pattern. Here's a quiz to help you begin:

Quiz—How Fat Are Your Habits?

Do you often find yourself watching the clock for mealtimes even when you're not hungry?

Do you try to skip meals and then end up eating twice as much because you're famished?

Do you find that you are reaching for second portions, when others at the table have eaten only half of their first?

Do you eat meals or nibble while reading, watching television or doing paperwork?

Do you sample and resample foods while cooking?

Do you finish leftover food while cleaning up after the meal?

Do you fill up on hors d'oeuvres at parties and then eat a full-course meal?

Do you eat everything offered at a restaurant because it "came with the meal"?

Do you keep nuts, chips, cookies, cake and other high-calorie snacks at home just in case you have "unexpected guests"?

Do you buy and prepare extra food for tomorrow's dinner only to find that you eat the extra before tomorrow comes?

Do you automatically add butter, gravies and sauces to everything just because they are served with the meal?

Do you "even out" the cake or pie by slicing off the uneven pieces and eating them?

Do you use "business" as an excuse to eat big lunches or dinners?

Do you comfort yourself with food whenever you are depressed, anxious, nervous, bored, worried, insecure or angry, and reward yourself with food when things go well?

Do any of these excuses sound familiar? "I was so good on my diet yesterday, I deserve a slice of cherry cheesecake today." "I was feeling so tired and depressed, I *needed* the chips and dip for energy."

A "yes" answer to any question is a warning flag of a behavior that "negatively" affects your eating and may be adding extra pounds. To restructure your eating habits for the better, try these tactics:

Eat slowly. One hypothesis is that it takes about 20 minutes for food in your stomach to send slowdown signals to the brain, so the slower you eat in the first 20 minutes, the more likely you are to feel satisfied before you reach for that second helping. If you need extra help to slow down, force yourself to put your fork or spoon down after each bite, or try eating with chopsticks or a cocktail fork.

When you eat, make it your only activity. You can polish off a whole bag of potato chips or bowl of nuts and not even realize it if you're reading or watching television at the same time.

If you cook extra for another meal, take out what you plan to serve immediately and put the remainder in the refrigerator or freezer *before* you sit down to eat.

If you can't resist eating the leftovers during clean-up after meals, make it a rule that everyone discards any leftovers on his or her plate before leaving the kitchen.

Leave high-calorie desserts and snack foods that you can't resist on your grocery store shelf. If you have to keep these foods around for other family members, buy flavors you do not care for. If you find yourself with leftover goodies after entertaining, you can freeze them, store them in the back of your highest kitchen shelf, or send extras home with your guests.

Start your meal with a low-calorie soup, raw vegetables, or a salad with lemon to slow down your eating and take the "edge" off your hunger before you reach the heavier parts of the meal.

Drink lots of a noncaloric beverage with your meals—water is great—to create a feeling of fullness.

Find other ways beside food to cheer yourself up when you are feeling low and to reward yourself when you deserve it. Eating fattening foods will only make you feel worse.

Exercise to improve your mood or reward yourself with a movie or other nonfood treat.

Don't eat when you aren't hungry. Don't eat simply because it's there. Don't eat because you paid for it. Don't eat because it's free. Don't eat to keep someone else company. Don't eat anything without asking yourself if you really, *really* want to. It's much easier to pass up food that you eat out of habit than it is to deprive yourself of foods you adore. Make every calorie count in enjoyment.

Final Words

Weighing In

Weigh yourself only once a week. Daily weigh-ins only set you up for disappointments. Many variables such as water retention, dehydration and even the time of the day can change your weight from day to day. But these changes don't reflect any true loss or gain of fat.

Expect Plateaus

No one loses weight in a steady, even pattern. *Don't be discouraged.* Plateaus are normal during the course of a diet. You may want to keep a graph of your weight loss so you can see any pattern in your plateaus as you progress through the diet. As you get close to your goal, weight loss will come harder. Lost pounds will have made your body smaller and, therefore, your caloric needs will also be smaller. This is a great time to burn up some extra calories by increasing your exercise.

Go Easy on Yourself

Getting rid of those extra pounds of fat on your body is hard enough without adding pounds of guilt to your psyche. Accept occasional slip-ups. Everyone overeats and underexercises sometimes. But just because you've cheated on your diet by eating a bowl of ice cream, doesn't mean that you might as well finish off the whole half gallon. The trick is to return immediately to your diet regimen—and to forgive yourself *completely.*

Then try to figure out how you can incorporate a small amount of ice cream into your diet—say, once a week—without exceeding the caloric level you've set for yourself. Dieting does not have to be an all-or-nothing situation. It's a system of tradeoffs. If you know a special occasion is coming up, you can avoid overloading by saving up calories beforehand. Cut back 200 calories a day Monday through Friday, and you'll have 1,000 extra guilt-free calories for weekend goodies.

V
*Plan Meals for
Your Needs*

Who Needs a Balanced Meal Plan?

Whether you're young or old, athletic or relatively sedentary, over-weight or underweight, planning your meals around the Basic Four and the Dietary Guidelines will keep you on the right track to a healthful diet that will meet your needs.*

You can personalize your meal plan by fitting it to your day's calorie quota. For those trying to lose weight, the suggested portions of the Basic Four provide an average of 1,200 calories per day—a good goal for weight loss. To maintain your present weight or to gain weight, just eat larger or additional portions from the first four groups and include some food from the "extra" group to reach your caloric goal.

Eat Well, Be Well® Sample Menus

To help you begin, we've planned two day's menus at different calorie levels for you, using the Basic Four as a guide and including some *Eat Well, Be Well*® recipes. Our menus (shown on pages 76–77) illustrate how different foods can be added to the basic 1,200 calorie diet to increase the caloric level to 1,600 and 2,000. Note that the amount of food specified for each caloric level builds on the previous caloric level. Notice, too, that since we chose the lower calorie selections within each food group, we had room for additional servings from some of the four groups and even some from the "extras" group. Our sample menus also demonstrate a model "breakfast on the go" meal and a model "dining out" meal.

These menus are just two examples of how you can get the recommended number of servings from the Basic Four Food Groups into your daily meal plan. These plans are only starting points; possibilities for modification are endless. If you need a little help, study the menu plan closest to the calorie level you wish to follow. If you are trying to reduce your caloric intake, be sure to read "Planning Your Personal Diet Strategy" on pages 61–66, too.

Making Up Your Own Menus

These meal plans are just examples; use them as an outline and adapt them to your own dietary patterns and include your favorite foods. When you make substitutions, try to choose foods from the same food group as those in the menu. That way your plan will also be balanced in terms of the Basic Four. Also remember to

---

*If you have any special health considerations, check with your doctor before making any major changes in your eating patterns.

watch your portion sizes unless you want to increase your caloric intake. *And don't forget to vary your choices daily to include a wide variety of foods within each food group, too.*

The sample menus feature three meals and snacks, but if you want to divide your food into five small meals a day, that's fine. Health professionals recommend that you space your calories throughout the day. People who eat only one meal per day tend to overeat at that meal, and their bodies may use the calories they consume less efficiently.

Combination Dishes

Most of us choose to combine foods from different food groups in appetizing combinations to add variety to our menu. Many of these combination dishes, such as pizza or tacos, fit into more than one food group, and the major ingredients can be assigned to specific food groups. A plain slice of pizza covers the Bread, Vegetable and Milk groups. Add meat and you have a serving from the fourth group as well. Here are some other examples:

Example 1:

A 1½-cup serving of Layered Beef and Eggplant Casserole (page 113) contains about 3 ounces beef + ½ ounce cheese + eggplant, tomatoes and onion.

Meat, Poultry, Fish and Beans	+ Milk and Cheese	+ Vegetables and Fruit
1 serving	⅓ serving	2 servings

Example 2:

A ¾-cup serving of Baked Vanilla Custard (page 173) contains 1 egg + ½ cup milk + flavorings.

Meat, Poultry, Fish and Beans	+ Milk and Cheese	+ Sweets, Fats, Alcohol
½ serving	½ serving	sugar

It is difficult to determine exact "portions" of all the different food groups included in certain mixed dishes, so often you'll have to estimate for yourself. To aid serious calorie counters, each recipe in this book provides the dish's calorie content per serving.

Eat Well, Be Well®—Sample Menu No. 1

—Featuring *Breakfast on the Go*—

1,200 Calories	1,600 Calories	2,000 Calories
Breakfast on the Go	**Breakfast on the Go**	**Breakfast on the Go**
Plain low-fat yogurt, 1 cup, with unsweetened pineapple, ½ cup, and toasted wheat germ, 2 tbsps. Coffee/Tea	Same	Same
Lunch	**Lunch**	**Lunch**
Turkey sandwich: Turkey, cooked, 2 ounces 1 large lettuce leaf Sliced tomato, ½ small Mayonnaise, ½ tbsp. Whole wheat bread, 2 slices Fresh orange, 1 medium Seltzer water with lime wedge	*Add:* *Minestrone, 1 serving	*Add:* Parmesan cheese, 1 tbsp. *Increase:* Turkey to 2½ ounces *Add:* *Minted Orange Lemon Ice, 1 serving (omit fresh orange) *AppleBerry Spritzer, 1 serving (omit seltzer)
Dinner	**Dinner**	**Dinner**
*Marinated Mushrooms, 1 serving *London Broil Pomadora, 1 serving *Rice Pilaf, ½ cup Steamed spinach, ½ cup *After Dinner Café, 1 serving	*Add:* Enriched French bread, 1 slice Margarine, 1 tsp.	*Increase:* *Rice Pilaf to ¾ cup, margarine to 2 tsps. *Add:* Strawberries, 1 cup Brown sugar, 1 tsp.
Snack	**Snack**	**Snack**
Skim milk, 1 cup *Peanut Butter Raisin Cookies, 1 cookie	Same	*Increase:* *Peanut Butter Raisin Cookies, to 2 cookies

*Recipes appear in Chapter VI

Eat Well, Be Well®—Sample Menu No. 2

—Featuring *Dining Out*—

1,200 Calories	1,600 Calories	2,000 Calories
Breakfast	**Breakfast**	**Breakfast**
Pink grapefruit, ½ *Nouvelle French Toast, 2 slices Maple syrup, 1 tbsp. Coffee/Tea	Same	*Increase:* Maple syrup to 1½ tbsps.
Lunch	**Lunch**	**Lunch**
*Vegetable-Stuffed Pita, 1 serving *Spiced Fruit Salad, 1 cup Skim milk, 1 cup	*Increase:* *Vegetable-Stuffed Pita to 2 servings	*Add:* 1% low-fat milk, 1 cup (omit skim milk)
Dining Out	**Dining Out**	**Dining Out**
Beef broth with mushrooms, 1¼ cups Flounder filet; baked w/butter, 4 ounces Baked potato w/chives and sour cream, 1 tbsp. Green salad, large with lemon wedge Honeydew melon, 1 wedge Coffee/Tea	*Increase:* Flounder to 5 ounces *Add:* French dressing, 1½ tbsps.	*Increase:* Flounder to 6 ounces Sour cream to 2 tbsps. French dressing to 2 tbsps. *Add:* Roll, 1 Butter, 1 pat
Snack	**Snack**	**Snack**
Rye crackers, 2 Swiss cheese, 1-inch cube	*Add:* Orange juice, 1 cup	*Increase:* Rye crackers to 4 Swiss cheese to a 2-inch cube

*Recipes appear in Chapter VI

Problem Solving Tips: For Dealing With . . .

Breakfast

It's difficult to perform at peak capacity unless you refuel after your night's fast, so don't set yourself up for a midmorning energy slump by skipping breakfast. But breakfast is also a meal that's easy to load with excess calories, fat and sugar; so don't *overdo* it.

A healthful, enjoyable breakfast depends on two things: knowing what type of foods can provide a good breakfast and being imaginative with them so you don't get stuck in the daily egg-for-breakfast routine.

Because a balanced breakfast should provide about one-fourth of your daily food needs, it's a good idea to select food from at least three food groups. But it's easy to follow that rule and still have lots of room for variety. Here are some suggestions:

If time is a problem for you, get breakfast organized the night before. Decide what breakfast will be and set the table before you go to bed.

For a breakfast to-go, measure your favorite hot cereal into a thermos; add boiling water, and close tightly. By work time the cereal will be cooked and piping hot.

Many delicious and nourishing breakfasts are fast and easy to prepare. Try plain yogurt or cottage cheese topped with fresh fruit and wheat germ or a frothy blender breakfast shake like our Coco-Banana Milk Shake (page 191) with a couple of breadsticks.

Top a slice of your favorite bread with an ounce of cheese and broil until the cheese is bubbly, or spread your toast with peanut butter and add sliced bananas or raisins.

If you usually grab breakfast on the way to the office, make your choices with care. A gooey pastry and coffee may help you curb midmorning hunger pangs, but these foods will give you a low nutritive return on your calorie investment. An English, corn or bran muffin with fruit and skim milk provide a lot more nutrition for about the same calories.

When weekends provide you with more time in the kitchen, make a batch of muffins (try our Banana Nut Muffins, page 168) and freeze them so you'll be set for the week ahead.

If you simply can't face any solid food early in the morning, sip a glass of juice when you first get up and then have a more substantial snack, such as cheese and crackers, or yogurt and a muffin as a midmorning break.

Be adventurous. Fish, chicken or last night's leftovers can provide a welcome change of pace and get you out of the early morning doldrums.

Lunch—At Your Desk or on the Go

When you're leading a busy life and there are a hundred things you want to get done in a day, lunch may often be a sandwich at your desk or a fast food meal. But if you make your choices wisely, a home-packed lunch need not be boring or unappetizing, and lunch at a fast food chain doesn't have to mean calorie overload. Here's how:

Bag Lunches

Sandwiches are often the No. 1 lunch choice because they can contain bread with servings of any (or all) of the other three food groups—meat, cheese and vegetables. Don't let yourself fall into the habit of having the same kind of sandwich day after day. Add variety with different fillings and different breads, such as whole wheat, rye, pumpernickel and pita pockets.

It's generally the filling, not the bread, that makes some sandwiches high in calories. Watch out for high-fat, high-calorie cold cuts and deli meats. Most commercially made salad fillings also have extra fat calories in the form of mayonnaise.

Lean roast meat and poultry are lighter alternatives. Also try the lean poultry alternatives to deli meats, such as turkey bologna, turkey pastrami and turkey ham. They taste like the real thing, but contain less fat and fewer calories.

Invest in a wide-mouth thermos for carrying hot, hearty soups and stews, or chilled salads and sandwich fillings. Try the *Eat Well, Be Well*® Split Pea Soup (page 95) or our Curried Chicken Salad (page 110). Great dishes like these make lunch a meal to look forward to—even at your desk.

If there is a toaster oven available, make a "tuna melt" by melting part-skim mozzarella cheese over tuna fish on rye bread. Top with sprouts, and you've got a balanced sandwich.

If you don't have an office refrigerator available, freeze a small can of fruit or vegetable juice at home the night before, and take it to work. It will be thawed but still cool by lunch and will complete a simple meal of cheese and crackers.

Check your daily diet to see if you, like many people, are often short on food from the milk and cheese group. It's easy to give yourself a calcium boost by rounding out our luncheon menu with a glass of milk. Remember that low-fat and skim milk have the same amount of calcium as whole milk, but less fat and fewer calories.

Fast Foods

The typical fast food meal of a deluxe burger, French fries and a shake totals close to 1,200 calories! Here are some tips to help you keep the calories in bounds.

Choose a plain burger (250 calories) instead of a deluxe burger (420–650 calories) or a fish sandwich (490 calories).

Go light on the condiments. Ketchup adds 15 calories per tablespoon. Tartar sauce is 75 calories per tablespoon, and mayonnaise comes in at 100 calories per tablespoon.

Add balance to the meal by asking for lettuce and tomato on your sandwich or burger.

Have a slice of pizza but avoid the extra high-calorie toppings such as pepperoni, sausage or extra cheese. Instead, ask for a topping of green peppers, mushrooms or onions.

Skip the thick shakes at 355 calories. They are usually low in milk but high in added fat. Stick with juice, diet soda, coffee, tea or, best of all, skim milk.

Choose a fast food restaurant with a salad bar and have a crisp salad instead of French fries with your sandwich, or make a large salad your main meal. Be liberal with the raw vegetables and conservative with the toppings and dressings.

Cut the calories from fried chicken by removing the fat-rich coating and skin and by choosing your extras carefully.

Have a taco. It contains foods from all four food groups and is less than 200 calories.

Skip the fruit pies at 300 calories and pick up a piece of fresh fruit on your way back to your home or office.

Remember *variety*. Don't have the same food every day.

Balance out your day's intake at other meals by focusing on the lower calorie selections in the food groups you didn't get in your fast food meal. Also, be aware that many fast foods are very high in sodium.

Remember *moderation*. Don't end up eating more food than you really want because your immediate hunger caused you to overorder. Keep your order small and then eat it slowly. Go back for seconds only if you are honestly still hungry.

Dining Out

If you are eating a special dinner at your favorite restaurant, the last thing you want to do is worry about the nutritional content of every morsel. So unless you're on a strict diet for health reasons or for weight loss—go ahead and enjoy yourself. But if you eat out on a regular basis, restaurant meals can be a stumbling block in your plans for moderation and balance.

It is possible to dine out and follow the principles of the Basic Four and the Dietary Guidelines if you exert a little control over how and what you eat. Here are some suggestions to help you with your dining-out dilemmas.

Select your restaurant with care unless you have terrific willpower; don't opt for a place that features an "all you can eat" buffet, family style service or fixed price complete five course dinners.

Ask for a salad with a lemon wedge or a low-calorie soup (broth-based) as soon as you sit down, so you won't fill up on bread and butter before your food arrives.

If you plan to have bread with your meal, take out what you want then have the waiter remove the bread basket and the butter from your table.

Be assertive when placing your order. Don't just smile at the waiter and let him douse your salad with dressing, heap your baked potato with butter, or pour gravy over your meat if you do not want the extra fat or calories. Make it clear that you want the dressing on the side, the potato plain and your meat served *au jus*. Then if the food doesn't come as ordered—send it back.

Keep portion sizes in check by ordering two appetizers instead of a full entree.

Dishes that require you to work before you eat will force you to eat slowly. Try whole artichokes, whole lobster or crab legs, whole fish, mussels or shrimps in the shell.

Consider carrying a "diet kit" in your purse or briefcase to make restaurant eating easier. Depending on your needs, your kit may include artificial sweetener, low-calorie or low-sodium dressing, and/or unsalted crackers or breadsticks.

If you are on a strict diet, try to look at the menu in advance so that you can plan what you are going to eat. If that isn't possible, call the restaurant ahead of time and explain your needs.

Select simple dishes such as lean meats, baked or broiled chicken or fish. If you don't know how something is prepared—ask. As a general rule, items described as buttered, fried, crispy, creamed or in a cream sauce, en casserole, in gravy, au gratin, in cheese sauce, escalloped, a la mode, au fromage, breaded, stewed, parmesan, with hollandaise, in pastry, batter dipped, prime or remoulade are high in fat and calories.

Don't feel that you have to eat every mouthful on your plate. Ask to have the leftover portion wrapped so that you can take it home to enjoy at another meal.

The best fat-free dessert choices are fresh fruits, fruit ices, fruit sorbets or angel food cake. To cut calories even more, skip dessert and have espresso with a twist of lemon. When you can't resist a rich dessert, share it.

If you treat yourself to an all-out splurge, enjoy it, then get back to your normal good eating habits (or your diet) the next day.

VI
Eat Well
Be Well® Recipes

Introduction

If you thought that balance and moderation in eating have to be plain, tasteless and dull, you're in for a surprise. On the following pages you'll find lots of delicious recipes all developed with the basic concepts of the Dietary Guidelines in mind (see Chapter II).

The *Eat Well, Be Well®* recipes include a wide variety of mouth-watering appetizers, hearty soups, salads, main dishes, breads and sandwiches, side dishes, beverages and even delectable desserts. Most recipes contain less fat, cholesterol, sugar, salt and calories than similar ones in many other cookbooks, but none of the *Eat Well, Be Well®* recipes skimp on flavor. Rather, they reflect moderation by using skim and low-fat milk and dairy products; lean cuts of meat, poultry and fish; low-sodium seasoning; and calorie-trimmed cooking methods. The results are nutritious recipes that the whole family will enjoy.

Remember that these recipes call for moderation—not elimination—so if you are on a special diet for medical reasons, they may not be appropriate for you. Please check with your physician or dietitian before including any of these dishes in your diet.

To help you fit these recipes into your individual meal plan, each includes its approximate calorie, protein, fat, carbohydrate, cholesterol and sodium content.

Turn the page and you'll see how easy and delicious it can be to *Eat Well* and *Be Well*.

Before You Begin

Seasoning With Spices and Herbs

Beef: Bay leaf, dry mustard, green pepper, marjoram, fresh mushrooms, onion, pepper, sage, thyme, beer or wine marinade, garlic

Chicken: Green pepper, lemon juice, vinegar, marjoram, curry, garlic, paprika, parsley, poultry seasoning, sage, thyme

Fish: Bay leaf, curry powder, dry mustard, green pepper, lemon or lime juice, marjoram, dill

Lamb: Curry powder, garlic, mint, mint jelly, pineapple, rosemary

Pork: Apple, applesauce, garlic, onion, sage, pepper

Veal: Apricot, bay leaf, curry powder, ginger, marjoram, oregano, basil

Asparagus: Garlic, lemon juice, onion, vinegar

Corn: Green pepper, pimiento, fresh tomato, lima beans

Cucumbers: Chives, dill, garlic, vinegar, lemon juice

Green Beans: Dill, lemon juice, marjoram, nutmeg, pimiento

Peas: Green pepper, mint, fresh mushrooms, onion, parsley, dill

Potatoes: Green pepper, mace, onion, scallion, paprika, parsley and vinegar or lemon if chilled

Rice: Chives, green pepper, onion, paprika, parsley, saffron, curry powder

Squash: Brown sugar, maple, cinnamon, ginger, mace, nutmeg

Tomatoes: Basil, marjoram, onion, oregano, scallions, dill

Soups: Bean soups—dry mustard, pepper; Vegetable soups—celery flakes, onion, garlic, basil, dill, red or green peppers, vinegar; Chowders—white pepper, onions, dried mushrooms; Split pea—bay leaf, parsley

Adapted from *Cooking Without Your Salt Shaker*, Dallas, TX: American Heart Association, 1978.

What to Do If You Don't Have...

For:	Use:
1 cup honey	¾ cup sugar + ¼ cup liquid
1 tablespoon cornstarch	2 tablespoons flour
1 cup cake flour	1 cup minus 2 tablespoons all-purpose flour
1 teaspoon baking powder	¼ teaspoon baking soda + ½ teaspoon cream of tartar
1 cup milk	½ cup evaporated milk + ½ cup water
1 cup buttermilk	1 cup milk + 1 tablespoon vinegar or lemon juice
1 ounce unsweetened chocolate	3 tablespoons cocoa + ½ tablespoon margarine

Measuring Simplified

3 teaspoons = 1 tablespoon
4 tablespoons = ¼ cup
5 tablespoons plus 1 teaspoon = ⅓ cup
16 tablespoons = 1 cup
2 cups = 1 pint
4 cups = 1 quart
2 pints = 1 quart
4 quarts = 1 gallon
1 fluid ounce = 2 tablespoons
8 fluid ounces = 1 cup
16 dry ounces = 1 pound
1 4-ounce stick margarine = 8 tablespoons
4 cups sifted flour = 1 pound
2 cups granulated sugar = 1 pound
8 ounce can = 1 cup
No. 303 can = 1¾ cups
No. 2 can = 2½ cups

Appetizers

NACHOS

4 corn tortillas
8 pitted black olives, sliced
¼ cup chopped Jalapeno pepper (about 1 large)
4 ounces Monterey Jack cheese, shredded (about 1 cup)

Preheat oven to 400°F. Cut each tortilla into 8 triangles; place on baking sheet. Bake about 5 minutes *or* until crisp. Sprinkle evenly with olives, peppers and cheese. Bake about 5 minutes longer, until cheese melts. Serve immediately.
Makes 8 servings, 4 nachos each.

Nutrients Per Serving:
85 Calories   5 grams Carbohydrates
4 grams Protein   16 milligrams Cholesterol
5 grams Fat   105 milligrams Sodium

STUFFED CELERY

1 cup low-fat cottage cheese
1 tablespoon chopped green onion (about 1 small)
1½ teaspoons Dijon-style mustard
1 small garlic clove, minced
4 celery ribs, each cut into four 2-inch pieces
Paprika

In small bowl, mix well cottage cheese, onion, mustard and garlic. Fill each celery piece with about 1 tablespoon mixture. Sprinkle with paprika.
Makes 4 servings, 4 pieces each.

Nutrients Per Serving:
50 Calories   4 grams Carbohydrates
7 grams Protein   2 milligrams Cholesterol
1 gram Fat   335 milligrams Sodium

MEXICAN DIP

¼ cup skim milk
2 cups low-fat cottage cheese
¼ cup finely chopped green pepper (about ¼ small)
1 cup chopped tomatoes (about 1 large)
2 teaspoons chili powder
⅛ teaspoon red pepper sauce

In blender container, process milk and cottage cheese until smooth. Stir in remaining ingredients. Cover and chill at least 1 hour. Serve with crisp crudités (carrot sticks, celery sticks, radishes, cucumber slices).
Makes 3 cups, ¼ cup per serving.

Nutrients Per Serving:
35 Calories	2 grams Carbohydrates
5 grams Protein	2 milligrams Cholesterol
1 gram Fat	160 milligrams Sodium

SPICY SHRIMP DIP

½ cup low-fat cottage cheese
¼ cup low-fat plain yogurt
2 tablespoons mayonnaise
1 2⅓-ounce can tiny shrimp, drained and coarsely
  chopped
2 tablespoons minced green pepper (about ⅛ small)
1 tablespoon chopped green onion (about 1 small)
1 garlic clove, minced
¼ teaspoon red pepper sauce

In medium bowl, with mixer at low speed, beat cottage cheese, yogurt and mayonnaise just until blended and smooth. Stir in shrimp, green pepper, onion, garlic and red pepper sauce and mix well. Serve with assorted crudités (carrot sticks, celery sticks, radishes, cucumber slices).
Makes 1 cup, 2 tablespoons per serving.

Nutrients Per Serving:
50 Calories	2 grams Carbohydrates
4 grams Protein	15 milligrams Cholesterol
3 grams Fat	95 milligrams Sodium

BAKED ARTICHOKE DIP

1 9-ounce package frozen artichoke hearts, thawed
⅓ cup part-skim ricotta cheese (about 2½ ounces)
¼ cup grated Parmesan cheese
2 tablespoons mayonnaise
⅛ teaspoon garlic powder
Dash ground red pepper

Preheat oven to 400°F. In blender container or food processor, process one-half of all ingredients until smooth, pushing mixture down with spatula, if necessary. Spoon into shallow 2-cup baking dish. Repeat with remaining half of ingredients. Bake about 30 minutes until lightly browned. Serve with crisp crudités (carrot sticks, celery sticks, radishes, cucumber slices).
Makes 1½ cups, 2 tablespoons per serving.

Nutrients Per Serving:
40 Calories
2 grams Protein
3 grams Fat
2 grams Carbohydrates
5 milligrams Cholesterol
60 milligrams Sodium

SHERRY CHEESE SAUCE

2 cups skim milk
⅛ teaspoon salt
½ teaspoon dry mustard
¼ teaspoon ground red pepper
Pinch nutmeg
2 tablespoons cornstarch
4 tablespoons sherry
3 ounces Gruyere cheese, grated (about ¾ cup)

In medium saucepan over high heat, combine milk, salt, mustard, pepper and nutmeg; bring to boil. In small bowl, combine cornstarch and sherry; stir until well blended. Stir cornstarch mixture into saucepan mixture. Reduce heat to low and cook until thickened. Remove from heat and stir in cheese.
Serve over vegetables.
Makes 2 cups, ¼ cup per serving.

Nutrients Per Serving:
85 Calories
5 grams Protein
4 grams Fat
5 grams Carbohydrates
15 milligrams Cholesterol
105 milligrams Sodium

MARINATED MUSHROOMS

½ cup water
⅓ cup red wine vinegar
1 tablespoon olive oil
2 garlic cloves, minced
½ teaspoon basil, crushed
¼ teaspoon thyme, crushed
⅛ teaspoon crushed red pepper
3 cups button mushrooms *or* halved medium mushrooms
(about 10 ounces)

In medium saucepan over medium heat, heat to boiling all ingredients except mushrooms; cover and simmer over low heat about 10 minutes. Add mushrooms; cover and continue to simmer about 5 minutes, *or* until mushrooms are tender, stirring occasionally. Transfer mixture to a medium bowl; cover and refrigerate about 2 hours, stirring occasionally. Before serving, drain mushrooms. Makes 1½ cups, ¼ cup per serving.

Nutrients Per Serving:

40 Calories	3 grams Carbohydrates
1 gram Protein	0 milligrams Cholesterol
3 grams Fat	10 milligrams Sodium

CRISPY HERBED PITA TRIANGLES

3 small whole-wheat pita bread pockets
4 teaspoons margarine, melted
¼ teaspoon oregano, crushed
⅛ teaspoon garlic powder
⅛ teaspoon pepper

Preheat oven to 400°F. Slit each pita bread pocket in half. Cut each half into 4 triangles; place on baking sheet. Combine remaining ingredients. Brush evenly over pita triangles. Bake about 10–15 minutes until crisp.
Makes 4 servings, 6 triangles per serving.

Nutrients Per Serving:

90 Calories	11 grams Carbohydrates
2 grams Protein	0 milligrams Cholesterol
5 grams Fat	45 milligrams Sodium

SPICY TOASTED PEANUTS

1½ cups wheat cereal squares
20 small unsalted peanuts
4 teaspoons margarine, melted
1 tablespoon Worcestershire sauce
¼ cup raisins

Preheat oven to 350°F. In a medium bowl, combine cereal and peanuts. Combine margarine and Worcestershire sauce; pour over mixture and toss well to coat. Spread mixture on baking pan. Bake until toasted, about 15 minutes. Stir in raisins.
Makes 1⅓ cups, ⅓ cup per serving.

Nutrients Per Serving:

150 Calories	23 grams Carbohydrates
3 grams Protein	0 milligrams Cholesterol
6 grams Fat	205 milligrams Sodium

POTATO WEDGES WITH CHEDDAR CHILI SAUCE

2 small potatoes (about 10 ounces)
4 teaspoons margarine
2 tablespoons all-purpose flour
½ cup skim milk
2 ounces Cheddar cheese, shredded (about ½ cup)
1 tablespoon chili sauce
Pinch ground red pepper

Cook unpeeled potatoes in boiling water about 20 minutes until tender; drain. Meanwhile, in small saucepan over low heat, melt margarine; stir in flour until smooth. Gradually stir in milk; cook, stirring constantly, until thickened and smooth. Stir in cheese, chili sauce and red pepper. Continue to cook over low heat, stirring, just until cheese melts. Preheat broiler if manufacturer directs. Halve potatoes lengthwise, then cut each half lengthwise into 3 wedges. Place on baking pan. Drizzle cheese sauce evenly over potatoes. Broil 3 inches from heat source about 4' minutes until lightly browned. Serve immediately.
Makes 4 servings, 3 wedges per serving.

Nutrients Per Serving:

175 Calories	18 grams Carbohydrates
7 grams Protein	15 milligrams Cholesterol
9 grams Fat	210 milligrams Sodium

PICKLED ZUCCHINI

½ cup water
½ cup cider vinegar
½ cup chopped onion (about ½ medium)
2 teaspoons mixed pickling spice
1 garlic clove, minced
2 cups sliced zucchini (about 2 medium)

In small saucepan, heat water, vinegar, onion, pickling spice and garlic to boiling; reduce heat to low and simmer covered about 10 minutes for flavors to develop. Add zucchini; continue to simmer covered about 5–7 minutes until tender crisp. Transfer to a medium bowl. Cover and refrigerate 2 hours.
Makes 2 cups, ½ cup per serving.

Nutrients Per Serving:

25 Calories	6 grams Carbohydrates
1 gram Protein	0 milligrams Cholesterol
1 gram Fat	3 milligrams Sodium

CORN AND PEPPER RELISH

¾ cup cider vinegar
¾ teaspoon mustard seed
¼ teaspoon celery seed
¼ teaspoon whole black peppercorns
⅛ teaspoon salt
2 cups frozen corn kernels
½ cup chopped green pepper (about ½ small)
¼ cup chopped red pepper (about ½ small)
¼ cup chopped onion (about ¼ medium)

In medium saucepan over medium heat, heat vinegar, mustard seed, celery seed, peppercorns and salt to boiling; reduce heat and simmer covered about 10 minutes for flavors to develop. Add vegetables; cook covered about 10 minutes until vegetables are tender crisp, stirring occasionally. Transfer to a medium bowl. Cover and refrigerate about 2 hours. Before serving, drain vegetables.
Makes 3 cups, ½ cup per serving.

Nutrients Per Serving:

60 Calories	15 grams Carbohydrates
2 grams Protein	0 milligrams Cholesterol
1 gram Fat	50 milligrams Sodium

Soups

BROCCOLI-CARROT BISQUE

1 13¾-ounce can chicken broth
2 cups broccoli florets (about ½ bunch)
1 cup sliced carrot (about 2 medium)
½ cup chopped onion (about ½ medium)
¼ teaspoon thyme
⅛ teaspoon pepper
½ cup skim milk

In medium saucepan over medium heat, bring chicken broth to a boil. Add the broccoli, carrots, onion, thyme and pepper and cook, covered, about 30 minutes until vegetables are tender. With blender at medium speed, puree one half of mixture. Repeat with remaining mixture. Stir in milk. Cook over low heat about 2 minutes until hot. Do not boil.
Makes 4 servings, ¾ cup per serving.

Nutrients Per Serving:

70 Calories	12 grams Carbohydrates
6 grams Protein	1 milligram Cholesterol
1 gram Fat	360 milligrams Sodium

SPLIT PEA SOUP

1 tablespoon vegetable oil
1 cup chopped carrot (about 2 medium)
1 cup chopped celery (about 2 medium ribs)
½ cup chopped onion (about ½ medium)
1 garlic clove, minced
8 cups water
2 cups split peas, washed and sorted
½ teaspoon salt
½ teaspoon thyme, crushed
⅛ teaspoon pepper

In large saucepan heat oil over medium-high heat and cook carrots, celery, onion and garlic about 5 minutes until tender. Add remaining ingredients; bring to a boil. Reduce heat to low; simmer, covered, about 1 hour; stirring occasionally.
Makes 8 servings, 1¼ cups per serving.

Nutrients Per Serving:

200 Calories	34 grams Carbohydrates
13 grams Protein	0 milligrams Cholesterol
2 grams Fat	180 milligrams Sodium

MINESTRONE

2 tablespoons vegetable oil
½ cup chopped onion (about ½ medium)
½ cup chopped celery (about 1 rib)
1 garlic clove, minced
1 16-ounce can whole tomatoes, crushed
2 cups water
1 cup shredded cabbage (about ⅛ small head)
1 cup sliced carrot (about 2 medium)
¾ teaspoon basil, crushed
1 bay leaf
¼ teaspoon salt
¼ teaspoon oregano
⅛ teaspoon pepper
½ cup ditalini *or* elbow macaroni
1 16-ounce can cannelini beans

In large saucepan heat the oil. Add the onion, celery and garlic and cook about 3 minutes, until soft. Add tomatoes, water, cabbage, carrots, basil, bay leaf, salt, oregano and pepper; bring to a boil. Reduce heat to low; simmer, covered, about 25 minutes. Add ditalini; simmer, covered, about 15 minutes longer. Stir in beans; cook 5 minutes longer, until vegetables are tender. Remove and discard bay leaf.
Makes 4 servings, 1¼ cups per serving.

Nutrients Per Serving:
270 Calories   40 grams Carbohydrates
  10 grams Protein   0 milligrams Cholesterol
   8 grams Fat   325 milligrams Sodium

COLD CUCUMBER DILL SOUP

4 teaspoons margarine
2 cups peeled, seeded and chopped cucumber (about 4
   small)
¼ cup chopped green onions (about 2 medium)
2 tablespoons cornstarch
1 13¾-ounce can chicken broth
½ teaspoon dill weed
⅛ teaspoon pepper
1 cup low-fat plain yogurt

In medium saucepan melt the margarine over medium-high heat. Add cucumber and onion and cook until onion is tender; stir in cornstarch. Gradually add chicken broth, dill weed and pepper. Stirring constantly, cook until mixture thickens slightly and begins to boil. Reduce heat to low; simmer, covered, about 5 minutes, stirring occasionally. Let cool and refrigerate until chilled. With blender at medium speed, process mixture until smooth. Using a whisk, add yogurt. Garnish with green onion, if desired. Makes 4 servings, ¾ cup per serving.

Nutrients Per Serving:

110 Calories	11 grams Carbohydrates
5 grams Protein	1 milligram Cholesterol
5 grams Fat	400 milligrams Sodium

MUSHROOM BARLEY SOUP

1 tablespoon vegetable oil
½ cup chopped onion (about ½ medium)
2½ cups sliced mushrooms (about ½ pound)
2 cups water
1 13¾-ounce can beef broth
½ cup barley
½ cup chopped parsley
1 bay leaf
¼ teaspoon thyme, crushed
¼ teaspoon rosemary, crushed
⅛ teaspoon pepper

In large saucepan heat oil over medium-high heat and cook onion until soft, about 3 minutes. Add mushrooms; cook about 4 minutes until mushrooms are tender. Add remaining ingredients; bring to a boil. Reduce heat to low; simmer, covered, about 1 hour or until barley is tender. Remove and discard bay leaf.
Makes 4 servings, 1 cup per serving.

Nutrients Per Serving:

155 Calories   25 grams Carbohydrates
5 grams Protein   0 milligrams Cholesterol
4 grams Fat   330 milligrams Sodium

NEW ENGLAND CHOWDER WITH SCALLOPS

4 teaspoons vegetable oil
½ cup chopped onion (about ½ medium)
¼ teaspoon thyme, crushed
2 small potatoes, peeled and diced (about 10 ounces)
½ cup chopped green pepper (about ½ small)
1 cup water
¾ pound flounder fillets, cut into 1-inch pieces
¼ pound bay scallops
2 cups skim milk
2½ teaspoons cornstarch
½ teaspoon salt
⅛ teaspoon pepper

In medium saucepan heat the oil over medium-high heat. Add onions and thyme and cook until onion is soft, about 3 minutes. Add potatoes, green pepper and water; bring to a boil. Reduce heat to low; simmer covered about 10 minutes until potatoes are almost tender. Add flounder and scallops. Cook, covered, about 8 minutes. Combine milk, cornstarch, salt and pepper; mix well. Stir into soup; simmer about 5 minutes, stirring occasionally, until fish is tender and soup is slightly thickened.
Makes 4 servings, 1 cup per serving.

Nutrients Per Serving:
250 Calories   23 grams Carbohydrates
  25 grams Protein   55 milligrams Cholesterol
  6 grams Fat   480 milligrams Sodium

CREAM OF CARROT SOUP

2 cups sliced carrots (about 4 medium)
1 12-ounce package frozen mashed squash
1 13-ounce can evaporated skim milk
⅛ teaspoon ground mace
⅛ teaspoon pepper
½ cup low-fat plain yogurt

In medium saucepan over medium-high heat, cook carrots in 1-inch layer of water until tender, about 10 minutes. Drain. Set carrots aside. In same saucepan, cook squash according to package directions, omitting salt and butter. In blender container, process carrots, squash and remaining ingredients until smooth. Return to saucepan and cook over low heat, covered, about 5 minutes until heated through. Pour into 4 bowls and top each with 2 tablespoons yogurt.
Makes 4 servings, 1 cup per serving.

Nutrients Per Serving:
150 Calories   27 grams Carbohydrates
  11 grams Protein   5 milligrams Cholesterol
   1 gram Fat   170 milligrams Sodium

RIBOLLITO SOUP

1 tablespoon vegetable oil
1 tablespoon olive oil
1 clove garlic, chopped
1 cup chopped onion (about 1 medium)
½ cup chopped celery (about 1 rib)
3 cups chopped leeks (about 2 medium)
2 cups chopped zucchini (about 2 medium)
½ cup chopped carrot (about 1 small)
2 cups chopped cabbage (about ¼ small head)
2 cups chopped tomatoes (about 4 medium)
1 teaspoon rosemary, crushed
⅛ teaspoon red pepper
1 pound dried white beans
1 13¾-ounce can beef broth
6 cups water
1 tablespoon Parmesan cheese

In large saucepan heat oils over medium-high heat. Add garlic, onions and celery and cook about 3 minutes. Add leeks, zucchini, carrots, cabbage, tomatoes, rosemary and red pepper. Cook about 5 minutes; add beans, beef broth and water. Bring to a boil and cover. Simmer about 1½ hours, until beans are cooked, adding water if necessary. Pour half the soup at a time into blender container and puree. Combine the two mixtures. Serve hot and sprinkle with Parmesan cheese, *or* refrigerate and serve cold.
Makes 8 servings, 1¼ cups per serving.

Nutrients Per Serving:

285 Calories	47 grams Carbohydrates
16 grams Protein	1 milligram Cholesterol
5 grams Fat	205 milligrams Sodium

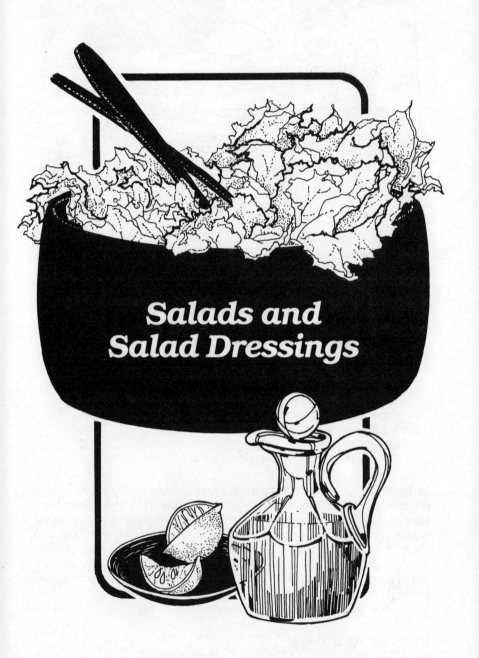

Salads and
Salad Dressings

BUTTERMILK HERB SALAD DRESSING

1 cup buttermilk
¼ cup low-fat cottage cheese
1 teaspoon dry mustard
1 tablespoon minced onion
1 teaspoon dill weed
2 tablespoons chopped parsley
¼ teaspoon pepper

In blender, process all ingredients until smooth.
Makes 1 cup, 2 tablespoons per serving.

Nutrients Per Serving:

20 Calories	2 grams Carbohydrates
2 grams Protein	2 milligrams Cholesterol
1 gram Fat	60 milligrams Sodium

GREEN GODDESS SALAD DRESSING

2 egg whites
½ cup chopped green onions (about 4 medium)
1 tablespoon chopped parsley
2 tablespoons tarragon vinegar
¼ cup vegetable oil

In blender, process until smooth all ingredients except oil. With blender running on low speed, slowly pour oil into mixture in a thin stream to make a smooth consistency.
Makes 1 cup, 2 tablespoons per serving.

Nutrients Per Serving:

70 Calories	1 gram Carbohydrates
1 gram Protein	0 milligrams Cholesterol
7 grams Fat	15 milligrams Sodium

CABBAGE SLAW

1 cup shredded green cabbage (about ¼ small head)
1 cup shredded red cabbage (about ¼ small head)
½ cup shredded carrot (about 1 small)
¼ cup chopped onion (about ¼ medium)
¼ cup raisins
½ cup low-fat plain yogurt
1 tablespoon fresh lemon juice
½ teaspoon dry mustard
½ teaspoon salt
⅛ teaspoon pepper

In large bowl, combine green and red cabbage, carrot, onion and raisins; mix well. Add remaining ingredients and toss to coat. Chill about 1 hour.
Makes 4 cups, 1 cup per serving.

Nutrients Per Serving:

65 Calories	15 grams Carbohydrates
3 grams Protein	1 milligram Cholesterol
1 gram Fat	305 milligrams Sodium

SPINACH ORANGE SALAD

3 cups fresh spinach (about 5 ounces)
½ head Boston lettuce
2 small oranges, peeled and sectioned
18 small walnut halves, chopped
2 tablespoons vegetable oil
2 tablespoons orange juice
1 tablespoon vinegar
¼ teaspoon salt
⅛ teaspoon pepper

In large bowl, tear spinach and lettuce into bite-sized pieces. Add oranges and walnuts. In a small bowl, combine remaining ingredients; pour over salad and toss gently to coat. Cover and refrigerate about 1 hour.
Makes 5 cups, 1¼ cups per serving.

Nutrients Per Serving:

155 Calories	12 grams Carbohydrates
3 grams Protein	0 milligrams Cholesterol
12 grams Fat	160 milligrams Sodium

ANTIPASTO SALAD

1 9-ounce package frozen artichoke hearts
3 cups lettuce leaves (about ½ head), torn into small
  pieces
½ cup sliced celery (about 1 rib)
½ cup chopped green pepper (about ½ small)
¼ cup chopped onion (about ¼ medium)
2 tablespoons roasted red pepper *or* pimento, cut into
  strips
¼ cup vegetable oil
2 tablespoons red wine vinegar
1 garlic clove, minced
2 teaspoons grated Parmesan cheese
⅛ teaspoon pepper

Cook artichoke hearts as label directs; drain and cool. Cut each artichoke in half. Place in a large bowl, with lettuce, celery, green pepper, onion and roasted red peppers *or* pimentos. In small bowl, combine remaining ingredients; pour over salad and toss gently to coat well. Chill about 1 hour.
Makes 6 cups, 1½ cups per serving.

Nutrients Per Serving:
165 Calories   8 grams Carbohydrates
  2 grams Protein   1 milligram Cholesterol
 15 grams Fat   75 milligrams Sodium

TABOULI

1 cup bulgur wheat
2 cups boiling water
¾ cup chopped onions (about ¾ medium)
½ cup chopped green onions (about 4 medium)
½ cup chopped parsley
1 cup cherry tomatoes, quartered
¼ cup fresh lemon juice
¼ cup olive oil
1½ tablespoons dried mint leaves, crushed
½ teaspoon salt

In large bowl, soak bulgur in water about 2 hours until soft. Add remaining ingredients and toss well. Cover and chill 1 hour.
Makes 4½ cups, ¾ cup per serving.

Nutrients Per Serving:

205 Calories	28 grams Carbohydrates
3 grams Protein	0 milligrams Cholesterol
10 grams Fat	185 milligrams Sodium

TANGELOSLAW

1 tablespoon vegetable oil
Grated peel of 1 fresh tangelo
Juice of 1 fresh tangelo (about ¼ cup)
1 tablespoon lemon juice
1 tablespoon honey
1 tablespoon toasted sesame seed
2½ cups shredded cabbage (about ¼ small head)
2 tangelos, peeled, sectioned, seeded, cut in half
3 tablespoons raisins

In jar with tight-fitting cover, combine oil, tangelo peel, citrus juices, honey and sesame seed; shake well. In large bowl, combine cabbage, tangelos and raisins. Toss with dressing; chill.
Makes 3 cups, ½ cup per serving.

Nutrients Per Serving:

90 Calories	15 grams Carbohydrates
1 gram Protein	0 milligrams Cholesterol
3 grams Fat	10 milligrams Sodium

TOMATO AND MOZZARELLA SALAD

4 medium tomatoes, sliced
2 ounces part-skim mozzarella cheese, thinly sliced
1 medium red onion, thinly sliced
2 tablespoons vegetable oil
1 tablespoon red wine vinegar
1 garlic clove, minced
¼ teaspoon basil, crushed
⅛ teaspoon pepper

On serving platter, arrange tomatoes, cheese and onion in overlapping layers. In small bowl, combine remaining ingredients and sprinkle over salad. Cover and refrigerate.
Makes 4 servings.

Nutrients Per Serving:

140 Calories	9 grams Carbohydrates
5 grams Protein	10 milligrams Cholesterol
10 grams Fat	75 milligrams Sodium

CRANBERRY ORANGE WALNUT MOLD

1 cup fresh or frozen cranberries
1½ cups low-calorie cranberry juice cocktail
½ cup orange juice
¼ teaspoon cinnamon
⅛ teaspoon ground cloves
2 teaspoons sugar
1 envelope unflavored gelatin
2 small oranges, sectioned and diced
12 small walnut halves, chopped

In saucepan, bring cranberries, cranberry juice cocktail, orange juice, cinnamon, cloves and sugar to a boil. Remove from heat; add gelatin. Stir until gelatin dissolves. Chill until mixture holds together loosely, about 1¼ hours. Stir in oranges and walnuts. Spoon into 3-cup mold. Chill until firm.
Makes 3 cups, ¾ cup per serving.

Nutrients Per Serving:

120 Calories	27 grams Carbohydrates
4 grams Protein	0 milligrams Cholesterol
3 grams Fat	10 milligrams Sodium

TACO SALAD

2 corn tortillas
1 pound lean ground beef
½ cup chopped onion (about 1 medium)
1 garlic clove, minced
1 8¼-ounce can whole tomatoes, chopped
2½ teaspoons chili powder
¼ teaspoon cumin
⅛ teaspoon crushed red pepper
⅛ teaspoon black pepper
1 8¾-ounce can red kidney beans
½ medium head iceberg lettuce, shredded
½ cup low-fat plain yogurt
2 ounces Cheddar cheese, shredded (about ½ cup)

Preheat oven to 400° F. Cut each tortilla into 8 wedges. Place on baking sheet and bake for about 10 minutes *or* until crisp. Remove from oven. In large skillet over medium heat, cook beef, onion and garlic until beef is browned, stirring frequently. Add tomatoes, chili powder, cumin, salt, red pepper and pepper; heat to boiling. Reduce heat to low; cover and simmer 40 minutes, stirring occasionally. Stir in beans; heat until hot, about 2 minutes. Place lettuce on large serving platter. Spoon chili over lettuce. Top with yogurt and sprinkle with cheese. Surround platter with tortilla chips.
Makes 4 servings.

Nutrients Per Serving:
480 Calories
  35 grams Protein
  22 grams Fat
36 grams Carbohydrates
90 milligrams Cholesterol
695 milligrams Sodium

SPICED FRUIT SALAD

½ cup canned pineapple chunks, packed in juice, reserve
⅓ cup juice
1 cinnamon stick
½ teaspoon rum extract
¾ cup sliced fresh strawberries
½ cup canned sliced peaches, packed in juice
½ cup cantaloupe balls

In small saucepan over medium heat, heat pineapple juice and cinnamon stick to boiling. Reduce heat; cover and cook about 5 minutes. Remove cinnamon stick. Add rum extract. In medium bowl, mix strawberries, peaches, cantaloupe and pineapple. Pour pineapple juice over fruit and toss. Refrigerate.
Makes 4 servings, ½ cup each.

Nutrients Per Serving:

60 Calories	15 grams Carbohydrates
1 gram Protein	0 milligrams Cholesterol
1 gram Fat	5 milligrams Sodium

SLICED BEEF SALAD

12 ounces sliced cooked lean beef (about 1 pound raw)
½ cup fresh bean sprouts (about 1½ ounces)
¼ cup sliced radishes (about 4 large)
2 tablespoons vegetable oil
1 tablespoon toasted sesame seed
2 teaspoons soy sauce
1½ teaspoons vinegar
½ teaspoon minced fresh ginger root
1 garlic clove, minced
⅛ teaspoon pepper

In medium bowl, combine beef, bean sprouts and radishes; mix well. In small bowl, combine remaining ingredients; pour over beef and toss to coat. Cover and refrigerate about 1 hour.
Makes 4 servings.

Nutrients Per Serving:

250 Calories	2 grams Carbohydrates
28 grams Protein	75 milligrams Cholesterol
13 grams Fat	290 milligrams Sodium

CURRIED CHICKEN SALAD

½ cup low-fat plain yogurt
1½ teaspoons curry powder
¼ teaspoon salt
⅛ teaspoon pepper
¾ pound cooked cubed chicken (about 1¾ cups)
¼ cup raisins
20 unsalted peanuts, chopped
2 tablespoons chopped green onion (about 1 medium)
Lettuce leaves

In large bowl, with fork, combine yogurt, curry powder, salt and pepper. Add remaining ingredients except lettuce; toss well. Cover and refrigerate 2 hours. Serve over lettuce.
Makes 4 servings, ½ cup each.

Nutrients Per Serving:

225 Calories	11 grams Carbohydrates
27 grams Protein	75 milligrams Cholesterol
8 grams Fat	230 milligrams Sodium

FOUR FOOD GROUP SALAD

½ cup fresh green beans (about 1 ounce)
½ cup chopped broccoli florets (about ⅛ bunch)
½ cup sliced carrot (about 1 small)
3 cups cooked rice, chilled
1 8¼-ounce can sliced red beets, drained and diced
½ cup minced onion (about ½ medium)
½ cup low-fat cottage cheese
6 ounces Cheddar cheese, shredded (1½ cups)
6 ounces cooked lean beef, ham, turkey *or* chicken,
    without skin, cut into strips

In medium saucepan over medium heat in 1-inch water, cook beans, broccoli and carrots until tender crisp, about 3–4 minutes. Drain and chill about ½ hour. In large bowl, combine all ingredients and toss.
Makes 6 servings, 1 cup each.

Nutrients Per Serving:

280 Calories	24 grams Carbohydrates
20 grams Protein	55 milligrams Cholesterol
12 grams Fat	340 milligrams Sodium with beef, chicken, or turkey 575 milligrams Sodium with ham

CHEESE AND FRUIT PLATTER
WITH POPPY SEED DRESSING

½ cup low-fat plain yogurt
¼ cup low-fat cottage cheese
1 tablespoon orange juice
1 tablespoon honey
1½ teaspoons poppy seed
12 green grapes
2 ounces part-skim mozzarella cheese, cut into cubes
2 ounces Cheddar cheese, cut into cubes
1 small apple, cored and cut into 8 wedges
   (about 4 ounces whole)
1 small pear, cored and cut into 8 wedges
   (about 5½ ounces whole)
½ small banana, sliced (about 2 ounces)

In small bowl, with mixer at medium speed, beat yogurt, cottage cheese, orange juice and honey until smooth. Stir in poppy seeds. On serving plate, arrange grapes, mozzarella and Cheddar cheese, apple, pear and banana. Serve with dressing.
Makes 4 servings.

Nutrients Per Serving:

205 Calories	23 grams Carbohydrates
10 grams Protein	25 milligrams Cholesterol
9 grams Fat	220 milligrams Sodium

Main Dishes

Beef

LAYERED BEEF AND EGGPLANT CASSEROLE

1 pound lean ground beef
¼ cup chopped onion (about ¼ medium)
1 garlic clove, minced
1 16-ounce can whole tomatoes, chopped, including
   liquid
1 teaspoon oregano, crushed
½ teaspoon basil, crushed
¼ teaspoon salt
⅛ teaspoon pepper
1½ cups peeled, thinly sliced eggplant (about ½ medium
   or ¾ pound)
2 ounces part-skim mozzarella cheese, shredded
   (about ½ cup)

In large skillet over medium heat, cook beef, onion and garlic until beef is browned, stirring frequently; drain and discard excess fat. Add tomatoes, oregano, basil, salt and pepper; heat to boiling. Reduce heat to low; cover and simmer about 20 minutes, stirring occasionally; drain and discard excess liquid. Preheat oven to 375°F. In 1½-quart baking dish, layer half of the eggplant, beef mixture and cheese. Repeat layers. Bake about 30 minutes *or* until eggplant is tender.
Makes 4 servings, 1½ cups each.

Nutrients Per Serving:
320 Calories   12 grams Carbohydrates
  26 grams Protein   85 milligrams Cholesterol
  19 grams Fat   400 milligrams Sodium

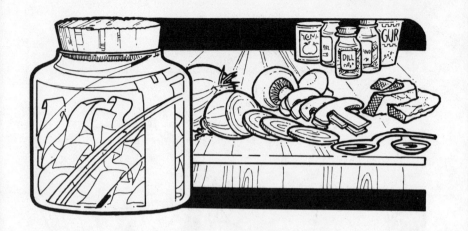

NOUVELLE BEEF STROGANOFF

1 pound lean beef round, cut into 2″ strips
2 tablespoons oil
1 medium onion, chopped
2 cups sliced mushrooms (about 6 ounces)
1½ cups beef broth
3 tablespoons all-purpose flour
2 tablespoons tomato paste
1 teaspoon dry mustard
¼ teaspoon oregano
¼ teaspoon dill weed
2 tablespoons sherry
⅓ cup low-fat plain yogurt

In skillet in hot oil, cook onions until translucent. Add beef and
mushrooms; cook until browned. Remove from skillet with slotted
spoon. In bowl, mix broth and flour; pour into skillet, stirring constantly until smooth and slightly thick. Add tomato paste, mustard, oregano, dill weed and sherry. Blend well. Add meat mixture
and cook 20–25 minutes until meat is tender and sauce is reduced.
In bowl, combine yogurt, and add 3 tablespoons meat sauce.
Reduce heat; slowly pour yogurt mixture into meat mixture. Simmer about 5 minutes. Serve with noodles or potatoes.
Makes 4 servings, about 1 cup each.

Nutrients Per Serving:
300 Calories   13 grams Carbohydrates
29 grams Protein   75 milligrams Cholesterol
13 grams Fat   470 milligrams Sodium

BROILED STUFFED HAMBURGERS

1 pound lean ground beef
2 ounces part-skim mozzarella cheese, shredded
   (about ½ cup)
2 tablespoons chopped roasted red peppers or pimentos
½ teaspoon oregano, crushed
⅛ teaspoon pepper

Preheat broiler. Divide beef in half. Shape one half into four patties.
Top each with an equal amount of cheese and roasted red peppers;
sprinkle evenly with oregano and pepper. Shape remaining half
beef into four patties. Top each filled patty with remaining patties;
press edges to seal. On rack in broiler pan, broil patties 3 inches
from heat source about 4 minutes; turn and broil about 4 minutes
more *or* until of desired doneness.
Makes 4 servings.

Nutrients Per Serving:

250 Calories	1 gram Carbohydrates
24 grams Protein	90 milligrams Cholesterol
16 grams Fat	105 milligrams Sodium

LONDON BROIL POMADORA

1 teaspoon dry mustard
½ teaspoon water
1 tablespoon vegetable oil
½ cup diced sweet red pepper (about ½ small)
¼ cup chopped onion (about ¼ medium)
2 tablespoons chopped hot chili pepper (about 2 small)
1 garlic clove, minced
1 8¾-ounce can whole tomatoes, drained and crushed
1 2-pound flank steak

In small bowl, combine mustard and water; set aside 10 minutes.
In small saucepan heat oil over medium heat. Cook red pepper,
onion, chili pepper and garlic about 3–4 minutes until soft. Add
tomatoes and cook stirring frequently, about 3–5 minutes until
heated throughout; set sauce aside. Preheat broiler. Place steak on
rack in broiler pan. Broil 4 inches from heat source about 8 minutes. Turn steak; broil 2 minutes. Spread reserved sauce evenly
over steak. Broil, 4 minutes more *or* until degree of desired doneness.
Makes 8 servings, 3 ounces each.

Nutrients Per Serving:

180 Calories	3 grams Carbohydrates
24 grams Protein	70 milligrams Cholesterol
8 grams Fat	80 milligrams Sodium

SCALLOPED POTATO AND BEEF CASSEROLE

6 new red potatoes, unpeeled (about 1 pound)
2 cups low-fat plain yogurt
1 cup low-fat cottage cheese
½ pound lean ground beef
½ cup beef stock
2 tablespoons chopped parsley
¾ cup sliced green onion (about 6 medium)
2 tablespoons all-purpose flour

Preheat oven to 350°F. In large pot in boiling water, cook potatoes until tender, about 20 minutes. Drain and slice. In blender container, process yogurt and cottage cheese until smooth. In large skillet over medium heat, brown beef, then drain off excess fat. Add beef stock, parsley, green onion and cook until onion is tender, about 10 minutes. Lower heat and slowly stir in yogurt mixture. In 1½-quart casserole dish, arrange potatoes and sprinkle flour on top. Pour meat mixture over top. Bake for about 30 minutes *or* until heated through. Then place under broiler about 2 minutes longer to brown top.

Makes 4 servings, 1½ cups each.

Nutrients Per Serving:

330 Calories   34 grams Carbohydrates
26 grams Protein   45 milligrams Cholesterol
9 grams Fat   465 milligrams Sodium

Seafood

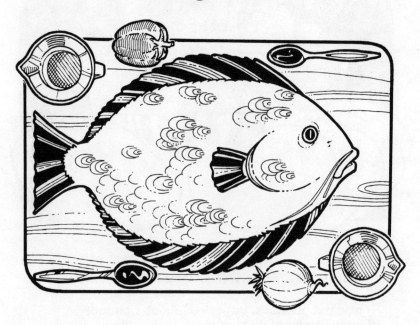

FLOUNDER WITH MULTI-COLORED PEPPERS

¾ cup fresh bread crumbs
¼ cup minced green pepper (about ¼ small)
¼ cup minced red pepper (about ¼ small)
¼ cup minced onion (about ¼ medium)
4 teaspoons margarine, melted
2 teaspoons Worcestershire sauce
⅛ teaspoon pepper
4 flounder fillets (1 pound)

Preheat broiler. In small bowl, combine bread crumbs, green and red pepper, onion, margarine, Worcestershire sauce and pepper. Arrange fillets on foil-lined broiler rack. Spread an equal amount of bread crumb mixture on each fillet. Broil 3 inches from heat source about 10 minutes *or* until fish flakes easily when tested with a fork. Makes 4 servings.

Nutrients Per Serving:

160 Calories	7 grams Carbohydrates
20 grams Protein	55 milligrams Cholesterol
5 grams Fat	205 milligrams Sodium

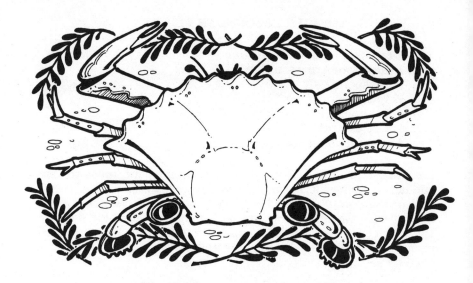

CRAB-STUFFED SOLE AU GRATIN

2 ounces Swiss cheese, shredded (about ½ cup)
½ cup frozen crabmeat, thawed and drained
   (about 3 ounces)
¼ cup low-fat plain yogurt
2 tablespoons minced green onion (about 1 medium)
2 garlic cloves, minced
¼ teaspoon salt
⅛ teaspoon ground red pepper
1 pound sole, cut into 4 fillets
½ cup dry white wine
½ cup water

In small bowl, combine half the cheese with the crabmeat, yogurt, onion, garlic, salt and red pepper. In center of each fillet, spoon an equal amount of crabmeat mixture; roll up jelly-roll fashion; secure with toothpicks. In large skillet, bring wine and water to boil. Add fillets. Reduce heat to low; simmer, covered, about 8 minutes *or* until fish flakes easily when tested with a fork. Preheat broiler. Gently transfer fillets to shallow baking dish. Sprinkle with remaining cheese. Broil 3 inches from heat source, about 3 minutes until cheese melts.

Makes 4 servings.

Nutrients Per Serving:

180 Calories	4 grams Carbohydrates
28 grams Protein	90 milligrams Cholesterol
5 grams Fat	315 milligrams Sodium

DEVILED FLOUNDER FILLETS

1 tablespoon dry white wine
1 tablespoon dry mustard
⅛ teaspoon salt
⅛ teaspoon pepper
4 flounder fillets (1 pound)
¾ cup dry bread crumbs
4 teaspoons margarine

Preheat oven to 500°F. In small bowl, combine wine, mustard, salt and pepper; set aside 10 minutes for flavors to develop. Brush mustard mixture evenly over fillets. Coat with bread crumbs. Line a baking pan with foil; spray foil with nonstick vegetable cooking spray. Place fillets on foil; dot evenly with margarine. Bake about 10 minutes *or* until fish flakes easily with a fork.
Makes 4 servings.

Nutrients Per Serving:

220 Calories	16 grams Carbohydrates
22 grams Protein	55 milligrams Cholesterol
7 grams Fat	345 milligrams Sodium

SHRIMP SCAMPI

2 tablespoons margarine
2 garlic cloves, minced
¼ teaspoon salt
⅛ teaspoon pepper
3 tablespoons dry white wine
2 tablespoons chopped parsley
20 medium shrimp, shelled and deveined (about 10 ounces with shell; 8 ounces cleaned)

Preheat broiler. In small saucepan over low heat, melt margarine. Add garlic, salt and pepper; cook about 3 minutes until garlic is tender. Stir in wine and parsley; cook about 2 minutes longer. Arrange shrimp on foil-lined broiler pan. Pour margarine mixture evenly over shrimp. Broil 3 inches from heat source, about 5 minutes until shrimp are pink.
Makes 4 servings.

Nutrients Per Serving:

115 Calories	2 grams Carbohydrates
11 grams Protein	85 milligrams Cholesterol
6 grams Fat	280 milligrams Sodium

HONEY-MUSTARD SCALLOP KABOBS

¼ cup dry white wine
1 tablespoon honey
2 teaspoons Dijon-style mustard
Dash ground red pepper
24 sea scallops (about 1 pound)
24 cherry tomatoes (about 1 quart)
2 medium green peppers, cut into 24 cubes
12 mushrooms, halved (about 6 ounces)

In small bowl, combine wine, honey, mustard and red pepper. Add scallops; toss to coat well. Cover and refrigerate 1 hour. Drain scallops, reserving marinade. Preheat broiler. On four 14-inch skewers, alternately thread scallops, cherry tomatoes, green pepper cubes and mushrooms. Place kabobs on foil-lined broiler pan. Broil 3 inches from heat source, about 8 minutes, basting with reserved marinade and turning occasionally.
Makes 4 servings.

Nutrients Per Serving:

150 Calories	16 grams Carbohydrates
20 grams Protein	40 milligrams Cholesterol
1 gram Fat	380 milligrams Sodium

POLYNESIAN SHRIMP

1 8-ounce can pineapple chunks in juice, drained,
    reserve liquid
2 tablespoons vegetable oil
1 tablespoon soy sauce
1 garlic clove, minced
¼ teaspoon ground ginger
⅛ teaspoon crushed red pepper
20 medium shrimp, shelled and deveined (about 10
    ounces with shell; 8 ounces cleaned)
1 cup chopped green pepper (about ½ small)
¼ cup chopped green onion (about 2 medium)
1 teaspoon cornstarch

Pour reserved juice into small bowl. Add 1 tablespoon oil, soy
sauce, garlic, ginger and red pepper; mix well. Add shrimp; toss
well to coat. Cover and refrigerate 1 hour, stirring occasionally.
Drain shrimp, reserving marinade. In large skillet over medium-
high heat, heat remaining 1 tablespoon oil. Add green pepper and
onion; cook about 3 minutes, stirring continuously. Add shrimp.
Cook about 3 minutes, stirring frequently until shrimp turns pink.
Combine cornstarch and reserved marinade; add to skillet with
pineapple; cook about 1 minute longer until thickened.
Makes 4 servings.

Nutrients Per Serving:
165 Calories   14 grams Carbohydrates
  11 grams Protein   85 milligrams Cholesterol
    8 grams Fat   420 milligrams Sodium

HALIBUT WITH MUSHROOMS IN CREAMY WHITE WINE SAUCE

3 tablespoons all-purpose flour
½ cup chicken broth
1 tablespoon margarine
¾ cup low-fat plain yogurt
¼ cup white wine
2 teaspoons grated lemon rind
¼ teaspoon pepper
1 pound halibut, cut into 4 fillets
1 cup sliced mushrooms (about 3 ounces)

Preheat oven to 350°F. In small jar, mix flour and chicken broth. Cover and shake until well blended. In medium saucepan over medium heat, melt margarine. Stirring continuously, slowly add flour mixture and cook until thick, about 30 seconds. Add yogurt, wine, lemon rind and pepper; stir until blended. Remove from heat. In baking dish, place halibut and surround with mushrooms. Pour sauce over all. Bake for about 30 minutes until done.
Makes 4 servings.

Nutrients Per Serving:
210 Calories
 28 grams Protein
  5 grams Fat
10 grams Carbohydrates
60 milligrams Cholesterol
230 milligrams Sodium

SALMON STEAKS WITH BROCCOLI SAUCE

4 salmon steaks (1½ pounds, 6 ounces each)
4 teaspoons margarine
2 tablespoons fresh lemon juice, divided
½ cup chicken broth
1 cup broccoli florets (about ¼ bunch)
¼ cup chopped onion (about ¼ medium)
1 garlic clove, minced
¼ teaspoon salt
⅛ teaspoon pepper

Preheat oven to 375°F. In shallow baking dish, arrange salmon steaks. Dot evenly with margarine; sprinkle with 1 tablespoon lemon juice. Bake about 20 minutes *or* until fish flakes easily with a fork. Meanwhile, in medium saucepan over medium heat, boil chicken broth. Add broccoli, onion and garlic and cook about 10 minutes until broccoli is tender. In blender at medium speed, process mixture with remaining 1 tablespoon lemon juice, salt and pepper until smooth. Serve sauce over salmon.
Makes 4 servings.

Nutrients Per Serving:

425 Calories	4 grams Carbohydrates
40 grams Protein	65 milligrams Cholesterol
27 grams Fat	415 milligrams Sodium

RED SNAPPER IN LIME VINAIGRETTE

½ cup dry white wine
½ cup water
1 pound red snapper fillets
¼ cup vegetable oil
2 tablespoons low-fat plain yogurt
1 tablespoon red wine vinegar
1 teaspoon fresh lime juice
1 teaspoon Dijon-style mustard
½ teaspoon basil, crushed
¼ teaspoon grated lime peel
⅛ teaspoon pepper

In large skillet over medium heat, heat wine and water to boiling. Add fillets; cook, covered, about 8–10 minutes *or* until fish flakes easily when tested with a fork. Remove fillets from skillet; cool. In medium bowl, combine oil, yogurt, vinegar, lime juice, mustard, basil, lime peel and pepper; mix well. Cut fillets into large chunks; add to dressing; gently toss to coat evenly. Chill 1 hour before serving.

Makes 4 servings, 3 ounces each.

Nutrients Per Serving:

240 Calories	2 grams Carbohydrates
23 grams Protein	60 milligrams Cholesterol
15 grams Fat	120 milligrams Sodium

SHRIMP CREOLE

4 teaspoons vegetable oil
½ cup chopped green pepper (about ½ small)
½ cup chopped celery (about 1 rib)
½ cup chopped onion (about ½ medium)
1 garlic clove, minced
1 28-ounce can whole tomatoes, chopped, including liquid
¼ teaspoon crushed red pepper
1 bay leaf
½ teaspoon thyme, crushed
20 medium shrimp, shelled and deveined (about 10 ounces with shell; 8 ounces cleaned)
1 tablespoon sherry
2 cups cooked rice

In medium saucepan heat oil over medium heat. Add green pepper, celery, onion and garlic and cook about 5 minutes, until tender. Add tomatoes and liquid, red pepper, bay leaf and thyme; heat to boiling. Reduce heat to low; simmer uncovered about 30 minutes, stirring often, until reduced slightly. Add shrimp and sherry; cook about 4 minutes longer until shrimp turns pink. Remove bay leaf and discard. Serve over rice.

Makes 4 servings, 1 cup each.

Nutrients Per Serving:

270 Calories	39 grams Carbohydrates
15 grams Protein	85 milligrams Cholesterol
6 grams Fat	360 milligrams Sodium

Pork

GINGER PORK

½ cup apple juice
1 tablespoon soy sauce
2 tablespoons diced fresh ginger
2 garlic cloves, minced
1 pound boneless lean pork loin, cut into ¼-inch strips
1 tablespoon vegetable oil
3 cups shredded Chinese cabbage (about ½
    medium head)
1 cup snow peas
1 cup mushrooms, sliced (about 4 ounces)
1½ teaspoons cornstarch

In medium bowl, combine apple juice, soy sauce, ginger and garlic. Add pork, toss well. Cover and refrigerate 2 hours, stirring occasionally. Remove pork from marinade, reserving marinade. In a large skillet over medium-high heat in hot vegetable oil, cook pork about 10 minutes, until tender. Remove pork from skillet. To drippings in skillet, add cabbage, snow peas and mushrooms; sauté until tender, about 5 minutes. Combine reserved marinade and cornstarch. Return pork to skillet along with marinade; cook about 1 minute *or* until slightly thickened.
Makes 4 servings, 1 cup each.

Nutrients Per Serving:
310 Calories   14 grams Carbohydrates
  26 grams Protein   70 milligrams Cholesterol
  17 grams Fat   430 milligrams Sodium

127

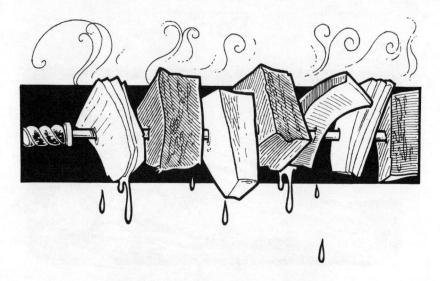

FRUIT-GLAZED PORK KABOBS

1 8-ounce can pineapple chunks in juice, drained,
    reserving liquid
4 teaspoons vegetable oil
1 garlic clove, minced
½ teaspoon ground ginger
¼ teaspoon salt
⅛ teaspoon pepper
1 pound boneless lean pork loin, cut into 1-inch cubes
1½ cups onion wedges (about 1 large)
1 cup green pepper cubes (about 1 small)
1 teaspoon cornstarch

Pour reserved juice into small bowl. Stir in oil, garlic, ginger, salt
and pepper. Add pork; toss to coat. Cover and refrigerate 2 hours,
stirring occasionally. Preheat broiler. Drain pork, reserving marinade. On four 12-inch skewers, alternately arrange onion, pork,
green pepper and pineapple. In small saucepan, combine cornstarch with reserved marinade. Cook, stirring, over low heat, until
slightly thickened. Place kabobs on foil-lined broiler pan. Broil
about 3 inches from heat source about 20–25 minutes, basting
with marinade and turning occasionally.
Makes 4 servings.

Nutrients Per Serving:
270 Calories   17 grams Carbohydrates
  20 grams Protein   55 milligrams Cholesterol
  14 grams Fat   190 milligrams Sodium

PORK ROAST WITH PIQUANT SAUCE

1 3-pound boneless pork loin roast, rolled and tied
2 garlic cloves, halved
¼ teaspoon pepper
1 cup water
¼ cup fresh lemon juice (about 2 lemons)
¼ cup dry white wine
2 teaspoons paprika
½ teaspoon salt

Preheat oven to 325°F. Place pork roast fat side up on rack in roasting pan. Rub garlic halves and pepper over pork; then mince garlic. Insert meat thermometer into center of roast. Roast about 45 minutes. In small bowl, combine minced garlic, water, lemon juice, wine, paprika and salt; pour over pork. Continue to roast about 1 hour and 15 minutes *or* until thermometer reaches 170°F. Place roast on serving platter. Let stand about 10 minutes before slicing. Skim excess fat from sauce. Serve sauce with pork.
Makes 8 servings, 4½ ounces each.

Nutrients Per Serving:
245 Calories   2 grams Carbohydrates
27 grams Protein   80 milligrams Cholesterol
13 grams Fat   200 milligrams Sodium

SZECHUAN PORK AND VEGETABLES

4 teaspoons vegetable oil
1 pound boneless lean pork loin, cut into ¼-inch strips
1 cup broccoli florets (about ¼ bunch)
1 cup red pepper strips (about 1 small)
¼ cup chopped onion (about ¼ medium)
1 garlic clove, minced
½ cup chicken broth, divided
1 tablespoon soy sauce
¼ to ½ teaspoon crushed red pepper
1 teaspoon cornstarch

In large skillet heat oil over high heat. Add pork and cook until meat loses pink color, about 2 minutes. Remove from skillet. To skillet add broccoli, pepper strips, onion and garlic; cook about 5 minutes until vegetables are tender crisp, stirring frequently. Return pork to skillet with all but 2 tablespoons of chicken broth, soy sauce and crushed red pepper; cook, stirring frequently, about 8 minutes. Combine cornstarch with remaining 2 tablespoons chicken broth. Add to skillet; cook, stirring 1 minute until thickened.

Makes 4 servings, ¾ cup each.

Nutrients Per Serving:

295 Calories	7 grams Carbohydrates
26 grams Protein	70 milligrams Cholesterol
18 grams Fat	530 milligrams Sodium

Poultry

CHICKEN, BROCCOLI AND PASTA CASSEROLE

1½ cups rotelle macaroni (about 3 cups cooked)
1½ cups broccoli florets, cooked (about ⅓ bunch)
12 ounces cooked cubed chicken
1½ tablespoons margarine
2 tablespoons all-purpose flour
1 cup skim milk
⅓ cup nonfat dry milk powder
1 teaspoon dry mustard
⅛ teaspoon salt
⅛ teaspoon pepper
4 ounces Cheddar cheese, shredded (1 cup)

Preheat oven to 350°F. Prepare macaroni as label directs; drain. Transfer to a large bowl. Add broccoli and chicken; mix well. In small saucepan over low heat, melt margarine; stir in flour until smooth. Gradually stir in milk, nonfat dry milk powder, mustard, salt and pepper; cook, stirring constantly, until thickened and smooth. Stir in all but 2 tablespoons of the cheese; continue to cook over low heat, stirring, just until cheese melts. Pour sauce over pasta mixture; mix well. Pour mixture into 1½-quart casserole. Sprinkle with remaining 2 tablespoons cheese. Bake about 25 minutes *or* until bubbly.
Makes 6 servings, 1 cup each.

Nutrients Per Serving:

370 Calories	31 grams Carbohydrates
29 grams Protein	70 milligrams Cholesterol
14 grams Fat	300 milligrams Sodium

CHICKEN COUSCOUS

1 tablespoon vegetable oil
2 cups cubed turnips (about 2 large)
1 cup sliced celery (about 2 medium ribs)
1 cup thinly sliced carrot (about 2 medium)
¼ cup chopped onion (about ¼ medium)
1½ pounds boned chicken breasts, skinned and cut into
   ¾-inch pieces
1 16-ounce can whole tomatoes, drained and crushed
1 13¾-ounce can chicken broth
½ teaspoon ground cumin
½ teaspoon ground cinnamon
⅛ teaspoon pepper
1 16-ounce can chick peas, drained
1½ cups precooked couscous

In large sauce pot over medium heat in hot vegetable oil, cook
turnips, celery, carrots and onion about 8 minutes, stirring frequently, until tender crisp. Add chicken, tomatoes, chicken broth,
cumin, cinnamon and pepper; heat to boiling. Reduce heat and
simmer, covered, about 25 minutes. Add chick peas; continue to
cook about 5 minutes longer. Meanwhile, cook couscous as label
directs. Remove 1 cup liquid from sauce pot; stir into couscous.
Spoon chicken mixture and liquid over couscous.
Makes 8 servings.

Nutrients Per Serving:
355 Calories   39 grams Carbohydrates
  30 grams Protein   50 milligrams Cholesterol
   4 grams Fat   350 milligrams Sodium

CHICKEN DUXELLE IN LEMON WINE SAUCE

4 teaspoons margarine
¼ cup chopped shallots (about 2 medium)
3 cups chopped mushrooms (about 10 ounces)
¼ teaspoon salt
¼ teaspoon thyme, crushed
⅛ teaspoon pepper
¼ cup chopped parsley
2 whole chicken breasts, boned and skinned, halved
    (1 pound boned and skinned)
½ cup dry white wine
4 tablespoons water, divided
1 tablespoon fresh lemon juice
¼ teaspoon grated lemon peel
1 garlic clove, minced
1 teaspoon cornstarch
Lemon slices and parsley for garnish

In large skillet over medium-high heat in melted margarine, cook shallots about 2 minutes. Add mushrooms, salt, thyme and pepper; continue to cook, stirring occasionally, about 20 minutes until all liquid has evaporated. Remove from heat. Stir in parsley. Meanwhile, on cutting board, with mallet, pound chicken to about ¼-inch thickness. Spoon an equal amount of mushroom mixture onto centers of chicken, leaving ½-inch border on all sides. From a narrow end, roll each jelly-roll fashion; secure with toothpicks. In large skillet, bring wine, 3 tablespoons of the water, lemon juice, lemon peel and garlic to a boil. Add chicken. Reduce heat to low; simmer, covered, about 20 minutes until chicken is tender. Remove chicken to serving platter. Combine cornstarch and remaining 1 tablespoon water; add to liquid in skillet. Cook, stirring, until slightly thickened. Spoon over chicken. Garnish with lemon slices and parsley.
Makes 4 servings.

Nutrients Per Serving:
200 Calories   8 grams Carbohydrates
  29 grams Protein   65 milligrams Cholesterol
   6 grams Fat   270 milligrams Sodium

CHICKEN WITH ORANGE GINGER SAUCE

¾ cup orange juice
½ cup chicken broth
2 whole chicken breasts (1 pound), boned, skinned
    and halved
½ teaspoon minced fresh ginger
¼ teaspoon salt
⅛ teaspoon pepper
2 small oranges, peeled and sectioned
2 tablespoons chopped green onion (1 medium)
2 teaspoons cornstarch

Set aside 3 tablespoons of the orange juice. Pour remaining orange juice into large skillet, set over medium heat. Add chicken broth and bring to boil. Add chicken, ginger, salt and pepper. Reduce heat to low; simmer covered, about 20 minutes *or* until chicken is almost tender. Add oranges and onion; continue to simmer, covered, about 5 minutes, until chicken is tender. Remove chicken and oranges to serving platter; keep warm. Combine cornstarch and reserved 3 tablespoons orange juice. Add to liquid in skillet. Cook, stirring constantly about 1 minute, until thickened. Spoon sauce over chicken.
Makes 4 servings.

Nutrients Per Serving:
190 Calories   14 grams Carbohydrates
  28 grams Protein   65 milligrams Cholesterol
    2 grams Fat   315 milligrams Sodium

STIR-FRIED CHICKEN WITH WALNUTS

2 tablespoons dry sherry
1 tablespoon soy sauce
½ cup plus 2 tablespoons chicken broth
1 tablespoon cornstarch
3 tablespoons vegetable oil
1 garlic clove, minced
1 pound boneless, skinned chicken, cut into pieces
1 pound snow peas
3 tablespoons chopped walnuts

In small bowl, mix sherry, soy sauce, ¼ cup chicken broth and set aside. Mix cornstarch with 2 tablespoons chicken broth and set aside. In wok *or* large skillet heat oil over high heat. Add garlic and cook about 30 seconds. Add chicken and cook until tender, about 3–4 minutes. Remove chicken with slotted spoon and set aside in warm dish. Add soy sauce mixture and snow peas. Cover and cook about 4 minutes until tender crisp. Stir in chicken, cornstarch mixture and walnuts. Cook about 30 seconds until sauce thickens. Serve over rice.
Makes 4 servings.

Nutrients Per Serving:

355 Calories	18 grams Carbohydrates
30 grams Protein	80 milligrams Cholesterol
18 grams Fat	550 milligrams Sodium

CRISPY BAKED CHICKEN

1 cup cornflakes, crushed
1 teaspoon rosemary
½ teaspoon pepper
1 cup skim milk
1 2½-pound chicken, skinned, cut into 8 pieces

Preheat oven to 400°F. In medium bowl, mix crushed cornflakes, rosemary and pepper. Dip chicken pieces into milk, then roll in crumb mixture. Place on foil-lined baking pan and bake about 45 minutes *or* until done.
Makes 4 servings, 2 pieces each.

Nutrients Per Serving:

210 Calories	9 grams Carbohydrates
27 grams Protein	75 milligrams Cholesterol
7 grams Fat	180 milligrams Sodium

CHILLED SLICED CHICKEN WITH MUSTARD SAUCE

1 cup low-fat plain yogurt
2 tablespoons skim milk
2 tablespoons chopped parsley
2 tablespoons chopped green onion (about 1 medium)
1 tablespoon reduced-fat mayonnaise
2 teaspoons Dijon-style mustard
⅛ teaspoon pepper
12 ounces cooked, cold sliced chicken (about 1 pound raw, boned and skinned)

In small bowl, combine yogurt, milk, parsley, onion, mayonnaise, mustard and pepper; mix well. On serving platter, arrange chicken. Spoon sauce over chicken.
Makes 4 servings.

Nutrients Per Serving:

210 Calories	6 grams Carbohydrates
28 grams Protein	80 milligrams Cholesterol
8 grams Fat	225 milligrams Sodium

CHICKEN AND SPINACH IN PHYLLO BUNDLES

2 tablespoons vegetable oil
2 tablespoons red wine vinegar
1 tablespoon fresh lemon juice
1 garlic clove, minced
¾ teaspoon basil, crushed
½ teaspoon salt
⅛ teaspoon pepper
2 whole chicken breasts (1 pound), boned, skinned
   and halved
1 10-ounce package frozen chopped spinach, thawed
4 sheets phyllo dough (strudel leaves), thawed

In medium bowl, combine oil, vinegar, lemon juice, garlic, basil, salt and pepper. Add chicken; toss to coat well. Cover and refrigerate 2 hours, stirring occasionally. Meanwhile, squeeze excess liquid out of spinach; set aside. Drain chicken, reserving marinade. Preheat oven to 375°F. Cover phyllo dough with plastic wrap to prevent drying. Remove one sheet. On center of smaller end, layer one quarter of the spinach; top with one chicken breast half. Fold longer ends toward center; roll up jelly-roll fashion forming an individual bundle. Place seam side down on baking pan sprayed with nonstick vegetable spray. Brush with reserved marinade. Repeat with remaining phyllo dough, spinach and chicken. Bake about 30 minutes *or* until lightly browned and chicken is tender.
Makes 4 servings.

Nutrients Per Serving:

290 Calories	19 grams Carbohydrates
31 grams Protein	65 milligrams Cholesterol
9 grams Fat	390 milligrams Sodium

STIR-FRIED POLYNESIAN CHICKEN

1 pound boned and skinned chicken breasts
2 teaspoons cornstarch
⅛ teaspoon pepper
2 tablespoons cold water
1 tablespoon soy sauce
1 8-ounce can sliced pineapple, packed in juice, quartered
    and drained, reserve ¼ cup juice
2 tablespoons vegetable oil
1½ cups thinly sliced celery (about 3 medium ribs)
1 cup thinly sliced onion (about 1 medium)
2 cups shredded green cabbage (about ¼ small head)
1 small clove garlic, minced
1 tablespoon minced fresh ginger
2 medium oranges, peeled and sectioned

Trim fat from chicken breasts and cut crosswise into ¼ inch slices.
Set aside. In small bowl, mix cornstarch, pepper, water, soy sauce
and pineapple juice. In wok *or* large skillet heat 1 tablespoon oil
over high heat. Cook celery and onions, stirring constantly, until
crisp tender, about 1 minute. Add cabbage and cook about 30
seconds more. Remove cabbage mixture and reserve. Add remaining tablespoon oil and heat to sizzling. Add garlic and ginger and
sauté about 30 seconds. Add chicken and cook about 3–4 minutes,
stirring constantly, until chicken is opaque and cooked through.
Stir in cornstarch mixture and cook until thickened, about 30 seconds. Stir in cabbage mixture, pineapple and oranges. Toss and
heat through, about 1 minute. Serve over hot rice.
Makes 6 servings, about 1 cup each (without rice).

Nutrients Per Serving:
200 Calories   18 grams Carbohydrates
  19 grams Protein   45 milligrams Cholesterol
    6 grams Fat   320 milligrams Sodium

CRAN-ORANGE GLAZED CORNISH HENS

2 1¼-pound Rock Cornish hens, skin removed
¼ teaspoon pepper
¼ cup cranberry sauce
½ teaspoon grated orange peel
1 garlic clove minced

Preheat oven to 375°F. Place hens, breast side up, in roasting pan. Rub evenly with pepper. Roast about 30 minutes. Meanwhile in saucepan over medium heat, cook cranberry sauce, orange peel and garlic about 3 minutes, until cranberry sauce melts. Brush hens evenly with sauce; continue to roast about 15 minutes longer until hens are tender. Makes 4 servings, ½ hen each.

Nutrients Per Serving:
200 Calories   7 grams Carbohydrates
26 grams Protein   80 milligrams Cholesterol
7 grams Fat   85 milligrams Sodium

TURKEY CURRY

2 cups cubed cooked turkey meat, skinned
    (about 1 pound raw)
2½ cups sliced mushrooms (about ½ pound)
⅓ cup chopped onion (about ⅓ medium)
1 tablespoon margarine
3 tablespoons all-purpose flour
1 cup chicken broth
1½ teaspoons curry powder
1 cup finely chopped unpeeled apples (about 1 large)
½ cup raisins
1 cup finely chopped parsley
¾ cup skim milk
½ cup water

In large frying pan, sauté turkey, mushrooms and onions in margarine until turkey is slightly browned. Stir in flour, chicken broth and curry powder; then add apples, raisins and parsley. Stir in skim milk and water. Simmer, stirring continuously, for about 3 minutes *or* until apples are tender.
Makes 4 servings, ½ cup each

Nutrients Per Serving:
295 Calories   31 grams Carbohydrates
28 grams Protein   55 milligrams Cholesterol
7 grams Fat   335 milligrams Sodium

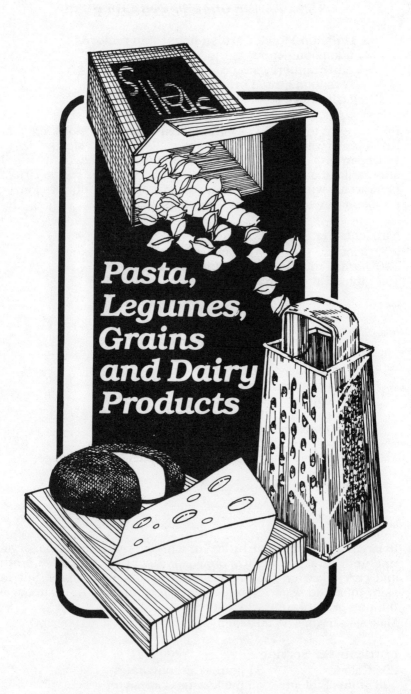

Pasta,
Legumes,
Grains
and Dairy
Products

FETTUCINE WITH PESTO SAUCE

¾ cup tightly-packed fresh basil
½ cup grated Parmesan cheese
2 tablespoons olive or vegetable oil
2 tablespoons water
12 small walnut halves
2 garlic cloves, minced
⅛ teaspoon ground pepper
4 ounces fettucine

In blender container *or* food processor, combine basil, cheese, oil, water, walnuts, garlic and pepper. Process, covered, until smooth and set aside. Prepare fettucine as label directs, omitting salt; drain well. Toss with prepared pesto sauce.
Makes 4 servings, ½ cup each.

Nutrients Per Serving:

305 Calories	25 grams Carbohydrates
10 grams Protein	35 milligrams Cholesterol
19 grams Fat	190 milligrams Sodium

LINGUINE WITH CLAM SAUCE

4 teaspoons olive oil
2 garlic cloves, minced
1 10½-ounce can minced clams, drained, reserve liquid
¼ teaspoon salt
⅛ teaspoon oregano, crushed
⅛ teaspoon pepper
1 cup cooked peas
4 ounces linguine

In small saucepan heat oil over medium-high heat. Add garlic and cook about 3 minutes until soft. Add clam liquid, salt, oregano and pepper; heat to boiling. Reduce heat to low and simmer, covered, about 5 minutes. Add clams and peas; cover and simmer about 5 minutes longer. Meanwhile, prepare linguine as label directs, omitting salt. Drain. Place in serving bowl, pour clam sauce over pasta; toss well to coat.
Makes 4 servings.

Nutrients Per Serving:

215 Calories	29 grams Carbohydrates
12 grams Protein	25 milligrams Cholesterol
6 grams Fat	605 milligrams Sodium

LASAGNA VERDE

1 tablespoon vegetable oil
2½ cups sliced mushrooms (about 8 ounces)
2 garlic cloves, minced
1 29-ounce can whole tomatoes, crushed
1 cup water
2 tablespoons chopped parsley
1 bay leaf
1 teaspoon basil, crushed
⅛ teaspoon pepper
2 tablespoons tomato paste
½ 16-ounce package spinach lasagna noodles
3 10-ounce packages frozen chopped spinach, thawed
15 ounces part-skim ricotta cheese (about 1½ cups)
½ pound part-skim mozzarella cheese, shredded
  (about 2 cups)

In medium saucepan heat oil over medium heat. Add mushrooms and garlic and cook about 5 minutes, until tender. Add tomatoes, water, parsley, bay leaf, basil and pepper; heat to boiling. Stir in tomato paste; reduce heat and simmer, covered, about 30 minutes, stirring occasionally. Remove and discard bay leaf. Meanwhile, cook lasagna noodles as label directs, omitting salt; drain. Preheat oven to 350°F. Squeeze excess liquid out of spinach. In 13-inch × 9-inch baking pan, spread ¾ cup of the tomato sauce. Arrange one-third of noodles in a layer over sauce; top with one-half of spinach, one-half of ricotta cheese, one-third of mozzarella cheese and one-third of remaining tomato sauce. Repeat layers of noodles, spinach, ricotta cheese, mozzarella cheese and tomato sauce. Top with remaining noodles. Spoon remaining sauce over noodles; sprinkle with remaining mozzarella cheese. Cover and bake about 45 minutes. Remove cover and continue to bake about 15 minutes longer until hot and bubbly. Let stand about 15 minutes before serving. Makes 8 servings.

Nutrients Per Serving:
330 Calories   34 grams Carbohydrates
 22 grams Protein   60 milligrams Cholesterol
 13 grams Fat   430 milligrams Sodium

PASTA FAGIOLI

4 teaspoons vegetable oil
¾ cup chopped onion (about ¾ medium)
¾ cup chopped celery (about 2 small ribs)
2 garlic cloves, minced
¼ cup chopped parsley
1 cup tomato sauce
1 cup water
⅛ teaspoon pepper
1 20-ounce can cannelini beans
1½ cups small shells

In medium saucepan heat oil over medium-high heat. Add onion, celery, garlic and parsley and cook until vegetables are soft, about 5 minutes, stirring occasionally. Add tomato sauce, water and pepper; heat to boiling. Reduce heat to low; simmer, uncovered, about 10 minutes, stirring occasionally. Add beans; continue to simmer, about 5 minutes longer. Meanwhile, prepare shells as label directs omitting salt; drain. Stir shells into sauce; cook about 5 minutes, stirring occasionally.

Makes 6 servings, 1 cup each.

Nutrients Per Serving:

245 Calories	42 grams Carbohydrates
9 grams Protein	0 milligrams Cholesterol
4 grams Fat	220 milligrams Sodium

PASTA PRIMAVERA

2 tablespoons olive oil
1 tablespoon vegetable oil
1 clove minced garlic
1 cup green beans (about 2 ounces)
1½ cups chopped zucchini (about 1 large)
1½ cups chopped broccoli (about ⅓ bunch)
½ cup fresh peas
4 cups ripe plum tomatoes, chopped (about 8 medium)
1 teaspoon chopped parsley
1 teaspoon basil
½ teaspoon thyme
1 teaspoon oregano
½ teaspoon pepper
¼ teaspoon salt
⅛ teaspoon crushed red pepper
⅓ cup Parmesan cheese
1 pound spaghetti

Heat oil in large skillet and sauté garlic, beans, zucchini, broccoli and peas about 2–3 minutes until tender crisp. Add tomatoes, parsley, basil, thyme, oregano, pepper, salt and red pepper. Simmer about 5 minutes until tomatoes are tender. In large pot, bring about 1 quart water to a rolling boil. Add spaghetti and stir to separate. Cook about 8–10 minutes until al dente (somewhat firm). Drain well in a colander and put pasta in large serving bowl. Add primavera sauce, and Parmesan cheese; toss and serve immediately.
Makes 6 servings.

Nutrients Per Serving:
425 Calories
16 grams Protein
10 grams Fat
70 grams Carbohydrates
3 milligrams Cholesterol
200 milligrams Sodium

SPINACH-STUFFED LASAGNA ROLLS

12 lasagna noodles (about 10 ounces)
1 10-ounce package frozen chopped spinach, thawed
¾ cup part-skim ricotta cheese (about 6 ounces)
1 egg, beaten
1 garlic clove, minced
1½ tablespoons grated Parmesan cheese
¼ teaspoon basil, crushed
⅛ teaspoon pepper
1 14-ounce jar spaghetti sauce
2 tablespoons water

Preheat oven to 350°F. Prepare lasagna noodles as label directs, omitting salt; drain. Meanwhile, squeeze excess liquid out of spinach. In medium bowl, combine spinach, ricotta cheese, egg, garlic, Parmesan cheese, basil and pepper; mix well. Lay noodles out flat. Spread an equal amount of spinach mixture over each, leaving 2 inches of noodle uncovered at one end. Starting at opposite end, roll up jelly-roll fashion. Pour ½ cup of the spaghetti sauce in bottom of an 8-inch square baking dish. Stand rolls upright in dish. To remaining sauce, add water; pour over rolls. Bake covered, about 30 minutes *or* until heated throughout.
Makes 6 servings.

Nutrients Per Serving:

305 Calories	44 grams Carbohydrates
14 grams Protein	100 milligrams Cholesterol
9 grams Fat	405 milligrams Sodium

PARMESAN NOODLE RING

8 ounces wide egg noodles
3 tablespoons margarine, divided
¼ cup chopped onion (about ¼ small)
1 cup sliced mushrooms (about 3 ounces)
½ teaspoon salt
¼ teaspoon thyme, crushed
⅛ teaspoon pepper
6 ounces finely chopped, cooked chicken (1⅓ cups)
¼ cup chopped parsley
2¼ teaspoons grated Parmesan cheese

Preheat oven to 375°F. Cook noodles as label directs, omitting salt; drain. In large skillet over medium-high heat, melt 1 tablespoon margarine. Add onion and cook about 2 minutes until soft. Add mushrooms, salt, thyme and pepper; cook about 4 minutes until tender, stirring occasionally. Melt remaining 2 tablespoons margarine. In large bowl, combine noodles, melted margarine, mushroom mixture, chicken, parsley and cheese; mix well. Spray 1-quart ring mold with nonstick vegetable cooking spray. Pack mixture into mold. Set mold in shallow roasting pan on oven rack; pour boiling water in pan to come halfway up sides of mold. Bake about 25 minutes *or* until heated throughout. To unmold, loosen edges with knife; invert onto platter.
Makes 4 servings, 1 cup each.

Nutrients Per Serving:

395 Calories	43 grams Carbohydrates
21 grams Protein	90 milligrams Cholesterol
15 grams Fat	430 milligrams Sodium

OLD FASHIONED MACARONI AND CHEESE

1½ cups elbow macaroni
2 tablespoons margarine
2 tablespoons all-purpose flour
1 teaspoon dry mustard
⅛ teaspoon pepper
1½ cups skim milk
⅓ cup nonfat dry milk powder
3 ounces Cheddar cheese, shredded (about ¾ cup)
1 6½-ounce can tuna in water, drained and flaked
2 tablespoons chopped pimento

Cook macaroni as label directs, omitting salt; drain. Preheat oven to 350°F. In medium saucepan over medium heat, melt margarine. Stir in flour, mustard and pepper until blended. Combine skim milk and milk powder until well blended. Gradually add to saucepan; cook until smooth and slightly thickened, stirring constantly. Stir in cheese until melted. In 2-quart baking dish combine cooked macaroni, cheese sauce, tuna and pimento; mix well. Bake about 25 minutes until bubbly and lightly browned.
Makes 6 servings, 1½ cups each.

Nutrients Per Serving:

280 Calories	30 grams Carbohydrates
18 grams Protein	30 milligrams Cholesterol
9 grams Fat	290 milligrams Sodium

CURRIED CHICK PEA CASSEROLE

3 cups cooked chick peas
2½ cups cold water
1 tablespoon vegetable oil
2½ teaspoons curry powder
½ cup chopped celery (about 1 medium rib)
¼ cup chopped onion (about ¼ medium)
2 garlic cloves, minced
1 14½-ounce can stewed tomatoes, drained and chopped
¼ teaspoon salt
⅛ teaspoon pepper
3 ounces part-skim mozzarella cheese, shredded
    (about ¾ cup)

In a medium saucepan heat oil over medium heat. Add curry powder and sauté about 1 minute. Add celery, onion and garlic; cook about 5 minutes until vegetables are tender. Add tomatoes, salt and pepper; cook about 5 minutes, stirring occasionally. Preheat oven to 350°F. Stir chick peas into tomato mixture with one-half of the cheese. Spoon into 1½-quart baking dish. Sprinkle with remaining half of cheese. Bake about 20 minutes until heated throughout.
Makes 6 servings, 1 cup each.

Nutrients Per Serving:
265 Calories   37 grams Carbohydrates
  14 grams Protein   10 milligrams Cholesterol
    8 grams Fat   360 milligrams Sodium

LENTIL AND VEGETABLE MEDLEY

2½ cups water
1 13¾-ounce can chicken broth
1 cup lentils, washed and sorted
1 teaspoon chili powder
½ teaspoon thyme, crushed
⅛ teaspoon pepper
4 teaspoons vegetable oil
½ cup chopped carrot (about ½ small)
½ cup chopped onion (about ½ medium)
2 garlic cloves, minced
1 cup chopped tomato (about 2 medium)

In medium saucepan over medium-high heat, heat water, chicken broth, lentils, chili powder, thyme and pepper to boiling; reduce heat to low, cover and simmer about 30–35 minutes until lentils are tender. Meanwhile, in large skillet heat oil over medium-high heat. Add carrot, onion and garlic and sauté about 7 minutes until tender. Stir in tomatoes; cook about 2 minutes more.
Makes 4 servings, 1½ cups each.

Nutrients Per Serving:
250 Calories   36 grams Carbohydrates
15 grams Protein   0 milligrams Cholesterol
6 grams Fat   340 milligrams Sodium

VEGETABLE BEAN STEW

¾ cup dry white beans
1¼ cups cold water
3 teaspoons vegetable oil
½ cup chopped onion (about ½ medium)
2 garlic cloves, minced
1 16-ounce can whole tomatoes, crushed
½ teaspoon thyme, crushed
½ teaspoon basil, crushed
¼ teaspoon salt
⅛ teaspoon crushed red pepper
1 cup sliced carrot (about 2 medium)
1 cup sliced zucchini (about 1 medium)
1 8¾-ounce can kidney beans

In small saucepan, soak beans in cold water overnight, *or* for quick method, heat beans and water to boiling. Cover and boil about 2 minutes. Remove from heat and let stand, covered, about 1 hour. Drain and measure soaking or cooking liquid and add enough water to make 1¼ cups. Return water and beans to saucepan; heat to boiling. Reduce heat to low; cover and simmer about 1 hour. In medium saucepan over medium-high heat in hot oil, cook onion and garlic about 3 minutes. Add white beans and bean liquid, tomatoes and seasonings; heat to boiling. Reduce heat to low; cover and simmer about 30 minutes. Add carrots and zucchini; continue to simmer covered about 30 minutes. Stir in kidney beans; cook about 5 minutes until beans and vegetables are tender.
Makes 6 servings, 1 cup each.

Nutrients Per Serving:
185 Calories   31 grams Carbohydrates
  10 grams Protein   0 milligrams Cholesterol
   3 grams Fat   345 milligrams Sodium

LIMA BEAN CASSEROLE

1 tablespoon vegetable oil
¼ cup chopped green onions (about 2 medium)
¼ cup chopped green pepper (about ¼ small)
½ cup shredded carrots (about 1 small)
⅛ teaspoon white pepper
¼ teaspoon basil
¼ teaspoon oregano
1 small clove garlic, minced
1 10-ounce package frozen baby lima beans, thawed
1 cup plain low-fat yogurt
½ cup grated mozzarella cheese (about 2 ounces)
1 tablespoon chopped fresh parsley
¼ teaspoon dry mustard
1 tablespoon bread crumbs

Preheat oven to 350°F. In saucepan in hot oil, sauté onions, green pepper and carrots until tender, 1–2 minutes. Add pepper, basil, oregano and garlic; blend well. Add lima beans and heat through. In bowl, mix yogurt, ¼ cup cheese, parsley and dry mustard. Add to lima bean mixture. Blend thoroughly. Pour into 1-quart baking dish. Mix remaining cheese and bread crumbs. Sprinkle over lima bean mixture. Bake covered about 30 minutes *or* until beans are tender and cheese melts.
Makes 2 servings.

Nutrients Per Serving:

385 Calories	44 grams Carbohydrates
23 grams Protein	25 milligrams Cholesterol
14 grams Fat	435 milligrams Sodium

VEGETABLE BURGERS

1 tablespoon margarine
¼ cup diced onion (about ¼ medium)
¼ cup diced celery (about ½ rib)
¼ cup diced green pepper (about ¼ small)
¼ cup diced red pepper (about ¼ small)
2 cups sliced mushrooms (about 6 ounces)
⅛ teaspoon pepper
1 cup low-fat plain yogurt
⅓ cup nonfat dry milk powder
1½ cups seasoned dry bread crumbs
2 ounces provolone cheese, shredded (about ½ cup)
1 egg, beaten

In large skillet over medium-high heat, melt margarine. Add onion, celery, green and red pepper; cook, stirring frequently, about 5 minutes, until soft. Add mushrooms and pepper; cook about 4 minutes longer, until mushrooms are tender; cool to room temperature. In small bowl, combine yogurt and nonfat dry milk powder, add to mushroom mixture along with remaining ingredients; mix well. Shape into 8 patties. Preheat broiler. Place patties on foil-lined rack in broiling pan. Broil 3 inches from heat source, about 6–8 minutes on each side.
Makes 4 servings.

Nutrients Per Serving:
325 Calories   40 grams Carbohydrates
 17 grams Protein   80 milligrams Cholesterol
 10 grams Fat   555 milligrams Sodium

BARLEY CASSEROLE

1 tablespoon vegetable oil
½ cup chopped celery (about 1 medium rib)
½ cup chopped green pepper (about ½ small)
½ cup chopped onion (about ½ medium)
1 garlic clove, minced
¾ teaspoon oregano, crushed
¼ teaspoon thyme, crushed
¼ teaspoon salt
⅛ teaspoon pepper
1½ cups barley
1 13¾-ounce can chicken broth
1½ cups water
3 ounces Cheddar cheese, shredded (about ¾ cup)

Preheat oven to 350°F. In large skillet heat oil over medium-high heat. Add celery, green pepper, onion, garlic and seasonings and sauté about 5 minutes until vegetables are tender. Spoon into a 1½-quart casserole. Stir in barley; mix well. Stir in chicken broth and water; cover and bake 1¼ hours until barley is tender, stirring occasionally. Raise oven temperature to broil. Uncover casserole; sprinkle with cheese. Broil 3 inches from heat source about 3 minutes, until cheese melts.
Makes 6 servings, 1 cup each.

Nutrients Per Serving:

275 Calories
   9 grams Protein
   8 grams Fat

42 grams Carbohydrates
15 milligrams Cholesterol
400 milligrams Sodium

RICE CON QUESO

4 cups water
1½ cups uncooked brown rice
½ cup dry black beans (1½ cups cooked)
½ cup chopped onion (about ½ medium)
3 garlic cloves, minced
4 ounces drained, chopped chili peppers (about ½ cup)
1 cup part-skim ricotta cheese
8 ounces Jack cheese, shredded (about 2 cups)
2 ounces Cheddar cheese, shredded (about ½ cup)

In medium saucepan, boil 2½ cups water. Add rice, cover and simmer about 10 minutes. Remove from heat and let stand covered about 15 minutes until all liquid is absorbed and rice is cooked. In another medium saucepan, add beans and 1½ cups water and bring to a boil. Reduce heat and simmer, covered, until tender, about 1½ hours. Preheat oven to 350°F. In medium bowl, mix rice, beans (including liquid), onion, garlic and chilies. Arrange rice mixture, ricotta cheese and Jack cheese in layers in a 2-quart casserole dish. Repeat layers, making sure to end with rice mixture. Bake about 1 hour. Sprinkle with Cheddar cheese and cook until cheese melts, about 5 minutes.
Makes 6 servings, 1 cup each.

Nutrients Per Serving:
460 Calories
23 grams Protein
19 grams Fat
50 grams Carbohydrates
20 milligrams Cholesterol
320 milligrams Sodium

RICE CRUST PIZZA

3 cups cooked brown rice
2 eggs beaten
1 15½-ounce jar pizza sauce
1 small green pepper, sliced into rings
¾ cup sliced mushrooms (about 3 ounces)
4 ounces shredded part-skim mozzarella cheese
   (about 1 cup)
½ teaspoon oregano, crushed

Preheat oven to 400°F. Spray a 12-inch pizza pan with nonstick vegetable spray. In a large bowl, combine rice and eggs. Spread onto pizza pan, making a ½-inch rim. Bake about 15 minutes. Reduce oven temperature to 375°F. Spread sauce over crust evenly. Top with pepper rings and mushrooms. Sprinkle with cheese and oregano. Bake about 10–15 minutes until cheese melts.
Makes 6 servings.

Nutrients Per Serving:

265 Calories
   10 grams Protein
   10 grams Fat

34 grams Carbohydrates
105 milligrams Cholesterol
430 milligrams Sodium

CRUNCHY APPLE RAISIN YOGURT LUNCH

2 tablespoons chopped dried apples
2 tablespoons nut-like cereal
1 tablespoon sunflower seeds
1 tablespoon raisins
1 cup low-fat plain yogurt

Mix together first 4 ingredients. Serve over yogurt.
Makes 1 serving.

Nutrients Per Serving:

280 Calories
   17 grams Protein
   5 grams Fat

45 grams Carbohydrates
5 milligrams Cholesterol
185 milligrams Sodium

CINNAMON RAISIN BLINTZES

1 cup plus 2 tablespoons skim milk
2 teaspoons vinegar
¾ cup all-purpose flour
2 eggs
1 tablespoon confectioners' sugar
½ teaspoon vegetable oil
1½ cups low-fat cottage cheese
¼ cup raisins
1 teaspoon honey
1 teaspoon vanilla extract
¼ teaspoon ground cinnamon
2 tablespoons margarine

In small bowl, mix milk and vinegar. Let set for about five minutes. In small bowl with mixer at medium speed, beat flour, milk mixture, eggs and confectioners' sugar until smooth. Cover and refrigerate 1 hour. Coat bottom and side of 7-inch skillet *or* crepe pan with vegetable oil. Over low heat, heat skillet; pour in scant ¼ cup batter; tip pan to coat bottom with batter. Cook batter until top is set and underside is lightly browned, about 3 minutes. With metal spatula, turn crepe and cook other side until golden, about 1 minute. Transfer crepe to wax paper. Add ½ teaspoon oil to skillet and repeat, cooking crepes until all batter is used. Stack with wax paper between each crepe. In small bowl, combine cottage cheese, raisins, honey, vanilla and cinnamon. Spoon about 3 tablespoons of mixture along center of each crepe; fold sides toward middle, then roll up in opposite direction. In large skillet over medium heat, in melted margarine, cook blintzes until golden, about 2 minutes. Makes 4 servings, 2 blintzes per serving.

Nutrients Per Serving:

310 Calories	35 grams Carbohydrates
19 grams Protein	140 milligrams Cholesterol
10 grams Fat	480 milligrams Sodium

Vegetables
and
Side Dishes

STUFFED CABBAGE

8 large green cabbage leaves
4 teaspoons vegetable oil
1 cup chopped green cabbage (about ⅛ small head)
¼ cup chopped onion (about ¼ medium)
1 garlic clove, minced
1 16-ounce can whole tomatoes, crushed
½ cup water
2 tablespoons tomato paste
¾ teaspoon ground cumin
⅛ teaspoon ground cinnamon
⅛ teaspoon pepper
2 cups cooked brown rice
2 ounces Cheddar cheese, shredded (about ½ cup)

In covered large skillet in 1-inch boiling water, cook cabbage leaves about 5 minutes; drain and set aside. In same large skillet heat oil over medium-high heat. Add chopped cabbage, onion and garlic and sauté about 7 minutes until tender. Remove from skillet and set aside. Add tomatoes and water to skillet; heat to boiling. Stir in tomato paste, cumin, cinnamon and pepper. Reduce heat to low; simmer, uncovered, about 10 minutes for flavors to develop. In medium bowl, stir together rice, cheese, reserved cabbage mixture and ½ cup tomato sauce. In the center of each cabbage leaf, place an equal amount of rice mixture. Fold 2 sides of leaf toward center; from narrow edge, roll up jelly-roll fashion and secure with toothpicks. Place cabbage rolls in skillet with tomato sauce. Over medium heat, heat sauce and cabbage rolls to boiling. Reduce heat to low; cover and simmer about 20 minutes, until heated throughout. Makes 4 servings.

Nutrients Per Serving:

280 Calories   39 grams Carbohydrates
    9 grams Protein   15 milligrams Cholesterol
  11 grams Fat   330 milligrams Sodium

BROC IN A WOK

1 tablespoon vegetable oil
⅛ teaspoon chili oil (optional)
2 cups fresh chopped broccoli florets (about ¼ bunch)
½ cup minced red pepper (about ½ medium)
2 tablespoons water

In a wok, heat vegetable oil and chili oil until they begin to sizzle. Add broccoli and pepper and stir with a wooden spoon in and out of the oil. Add water and cook, covered, about 1 minute, stirring occasionally. Serve immediately.
Makes 2 servings.

Nutrients Per Serving:

115 Calories   10 grams Carbohydrates
  5 grams Protein   0 milligrams Cholesterol
  8 grams Fat   35 milligrams Sodium

GARDEN CURRY

2 tablespoons vegetable oil
1 tablespoon curry powder
2 cups broccoli florets (about ½ bunch)
1 cup sliced zucchini (about 1 medium)
1 cup diagonally sliced carrot (about 2 medium)
1 cup sweet red pepper strips (about 1 small)
½ cup and 2 tablespoons chicken broth
⅛ teaspoon pepper
1 10-ounce package frozen corn, thawed
1 small apple, cored and cut into 8 wedges
1 tablespoon cornstarch

In large saucepan heat oil over medium heat. Add curry powder and cook 1 minute. Add broccoli, zucchini, carrot, red pepper, ½ cup of the chicken broth and pepper; heat to boiling. Reduce heat and simmer, covered, about 15 minutes. Add corn and apple; continue to cook, covered, about 5 minutes or until vegetables are tender crisp. Combine cornstarch and remaining 2 tablespoons of the chicken broth. Add to skillet. Cook and stir about 1 minute until thickened.
Makes 4 servings, 1 cup each.

Nutrients Per Serving:

210 Calories   32 grams Carbohydrates
  7 grams Protein   0 milligrams Cholesterol
  8 grams Fat   170 milligrams Sodium

RATATOUILLE-STUFFED PEPPERS

4 teaspoons vegetable oil
1 cup chopped eggplant (about ⅓ medium or ½ pound)
¾ cup chopped tomato (about 1 large)
¾ cup chopped green pepper (about ¼ small)
½ cup sliced zucchini, halved (about ½ medium)
½ cup chopped onion (about ½ medium)
2 garlic cloves, minced
¾ teaspoon basil, crushed
¼ teaspoon oregano, crushed
⅛ teaspoon salt
⅛ teaspoon pepper
4 small green peppers
1 teaspoon grated Parmesan cheese

In medium saucepan heat oil over medium-high heat. Add all ingredients except whole green peppers and cheese and cook about 10 minutes, covered, stirring frequently. Remove cover and continue to cook about 5 minutes longer. Meanwhile, remove top quarter of peppers; core and remove seeds. Parboil peppers in boiling water to cover about 6 minutes until tender crisp; drain. Preheat broiler. Spoon an equal amount of vegetable mixture into each pepper; sprinkle each with ¼ teaspoon cheese. Place on broiler rack; broil 3 inches from heat source about 2 minutes.
Makes 4 servings.

Nutrients Per Serving:
95 Calories   11 grams Carbohydrates
 3 grams Protein   1 milligram Cholesterol
 5 grams Fat   95 milligrams Sodium

BULGUR-STUFFED ACORN SQUASH

1⅓ cups boiling water
⅔ cup bulgur *or* cracked wheat (2 cups after soaking)
4 teaspoons vegetable oil
¼ cup chopped carrot (about ½ small)
2 tablespoons chopped onion (about ⅛ medium)
2 garlic clove, minced
1 cup chopped mushrooms (about 3 ounces)
1 teaspoon basil, crushed
½ teaspoon salt
¼ teaspoon pepper
⅛ teaspoon rosemary, crushed
2 eggs, beaten
1 tablespoon dry white wine
2 small acorn squash, halved lengthwise and seeded
½ cup low-fat plain yogurt

In medium bowl, combine boiling water and bulgur; set aside 2 hours until liquid is absorbed. In large skillet heat oil over medium-high heat. Add carrot, onion, and garlic and sauté about 3 minutes. Add mushrooms, basil, salt, pepper and rosemary; cook, stirring occasionally, about 4 minutes until vegetables are tender. Stir in eggs; cook, stirring occasionally until eggs are cooked. Add wine; cook about 1 minute. Add cooked mixture to bulgur; mix well. Preheat oven to 375°F. Place squash, cut side up, in 9-inch square baking dish. Into each half, spoon an equal amount of bulgur mixture. Pour 1 cup water into bottom of dish. Cover and bake about 1 hour *or* until squash is fork tender. Serve each with 2 tablespoons yogurt.
Makes 4 servings.

Nutrients Per Serving:

300 Calories	49 grams Carbohydrates
11 grams Protein	140 milligrams Cholesterol
8 grams Fat	335 milligrams Sodium

OVEN-FRIED TOMATO SLICES

⅓ cup dry bread crumbs
1 tablespoon grated Parmesan cheese
⅛ teaspoon oregano
Dash pepper
Dash garlic powder
4 medium tomatoes, sliced
1 tablespoon margarine, melted

Preheat oven to 400°F. In shallow dish, combine bread crumbs, cheese, oregano, pepper and garlic powder; mix well. Coat tomato slices evenly with crumbs. Spray baking sheet with nonstick vegetable spray. Place tomato slices on baking sheet. Drizzle evenly with margarine. Bake about 5 minutes until tomatoes are tender. Heat broiler. Place tomatoes under broiler and broil about 2 minutes until lightly browned.
Makes 4 servings.

Nutrients Per Serving:

90 Calories
3 grams Protein
4 grams Fat
11 grams Carbohydrates
1 milligram Cholesterol
120 milligrams Sodium

RICE PILAF

1 tablespoon vegetable oil
¼ cup minced onion (about ¼ medium)
¼ cup minced green pepper (about ¼ small)
¼ cup minced red pepper (about ¼ small)
¼ cup minced celery (about ½ rib)
1 cup chicken broth
½ teaspoon oregano, crushed
⅛ teaspoon pepper
½ cup converted white rice

In small saucepan heat oil over medium-high heat. Add onion, green and red pepper, and celery and sauté about 4 minutes until tender. Add chicken broth, oregano and pepper; heat to boiling. Add rice; reduce heat to low; cover and simmer about 20 minutes *or* until tender.
Makes 4 servings, ½ cup each.

Nutrients Per Serving:

140 Calories
4 grams Protein
4 grams Fat
21 grams Carbohydrates
0 milligrams Cholesterol
220 milligrams Sodium

SAUTÉED SNOW PEAS AND CUCUMBERS

1¼ teaspoons vegetable oil
1 teaspoon margarine
¼ cup chopped onion (about ¼ small)
1 garlic clove minced
1 cup snow peas
1 cup peeled, seeded and chopped cucumber (about 2
    small)
1 tablespoon toasted sesame seeds
½ teaspoon ground ginger
¼ teaspoon salt
⅛ teaspoon pepper

In large skillet heat oil and margarine over medium heat. Add onion and garlic and sauté about 3 minutes until soft. Add remaining ingredients; sauté about 5 minutes until vegetables are tender crisp.
Makes 4 servings, ½ cup each.

Nutrients Per Serving:

65 Calories	8 grams Carbohydrates
2 grams Protein	0 milligrams Cholesterol
4 grams Fat	150 milligrams Sodium

YOGURT-TOPPED POTATOES

4 small potatoes (about 1¼ pounds)
½ cup low-fat plain yogurt
1 ounce Cheddar cheese, shredded (about ¼ cup)
1 teaspoon chopped chives

Preheat oven to 450°F. Wash and dry potatoes, pierce with a fork. Bake on oven rack about 45 minutes *or* until fork tender. Cut each potato in half lengthwise without cutting all the way through the bottom. Top each with 2 tablespoons yogurt, 1 tablespoon cheese and ¼ teaspoon chives.
Makes 4 servings.

Nutrients Per Serving:

150 Calories	27 grams Carbohydrates
6 grams Protein	10 milligrams Cholesterol
3 grams Fat	70 milligrams Sodium

HERB-SEASONED POTATOES

6 cups cubed potatoes (about 6–8 medium)
½ cup sliced onions (about ½ medium)
2 teaspoons dried parsley flakes
½ teaspoon all-purpose flour
⅛ teaspoon thyme
1 egg, beaten
Dash white pepper

In saucepan, cover potatoes and onions with water. Simmer until tender, about 20 minutes. Drain, reserving ½ cup liquid. Transfer potatoes and onions to large bowl. In saucepan, combine potato liquid, parsley, flour and thyme. Simmer until smooth and slightly thickened. Reduce heat and add egg, stirring constantly, until mixture becomes light yellow in color. Season with pepper. Pour sauce over potatoes and mix well.
Makes 12 servings, ½ cup each.

Nutrients Per Serving:
70 Calories   15 grams Carbohydrates
  2 grams Protein   25 milligrams Cholesterol
  1 gram Fat   10 milligrams Sodium

LEMON-GARLIC BRUSSELS SPROUTS AND CARROTS

1 tablespoon margarine
2 10-ounce packages frozen Brussels sprouts, thawed
    and halved (about 3 cups)
1 cup julienne cut carrot (about 2 medium)
1 garlic clove, minced
¾ teaspoon basil, crushed
⅛ teaspoon pepper
1 tablespoon fresh lemon juice

In large skillet over medium heat, melt margarine. Add Brussels sprouts, carrots, garlic, basil and pepper; sauté about 7 minutes until tender, stirring frequently. Stir in lemon juice; cook about 2 minutes longer, stirring occasionally.
Makes 6 servings, ⅔ cup each.

Nutrients Per Serving:
60 Calories   9 grams Carbohydrates
  3 grams Protein   0 milligrams Cholesterol
  2 grams Fat   45 milligrams Sodium

Breads and Sandwiches

NOUVELLE FRENCH TOAST

2 slices whole-wheat bread
2 egg whites
2 tablespoons skim milk
¼ teaspoon vanilla
⅛ teaspoon cinnamon
1½ teaspoons vegetable oil

In small bowl, combine egg whites, skim milk, vanilla and cinnamon and beat lightly. Heat a griddle *or* heavy frying pan until hot and add oil. Dip bread into egg white mixture; fry until golden brown for about 1 minute on both sides. Remove from the griddle and serve immediately.
Makes 2 servings.

Nutrients Per Serving:
110 Calories   12 grams Carbohydrates
6 grams Protein   1 milligram Cholesterol
4 grams Fat   180 milligrams Sodium

SPICED POPOVERS

2 eggs
1 cup skim milk
½ cup all-purpose flour
½ cup whole-wheat flour
1 teaspoon vegetable oil
¾ teaspoon ground cinnamon

Preheat oven to 450°F. Spray 4 10-ounce custard cups with non-stick vegetable spray. In medium bowl with mixer at low speed, beat eggs until frothy; beat in milk, flour, oil and cinnamon until blended. Fill custard cups half full. Bake about 50 minutes. Let cool and carefully remove from custard cups.
Makes 4 servings.

Nutrients Per Serving:
180 Calories   26 grams Carbohydrates
9 grams Protein   140 milligrams Cholesterol
5 grams Fat   70 milligrams Sodium

RAISIN BRAN QUICK BREAD

1½ cups all-purpose flour
1 cup unprocessed bran
¼ cup sugar
2 teaspoons baking powder
¾ teaspoon ground cinnamon
¼ teaspoon ground nutmeg
¼ teaspoon baking soda
⅔ cup skim milk
8 tablespoons vegetable oil
2 eggs
1 cup raisins

Preheat oven to 350°F. In a large bowl with fork, mix flour, bran, sugar, baking powder, cinnamon, nutmeg and baking soda. In a small bowl with fork, beat together milk, oil and eggs; add to flour mixture and stir until well mixed. Stir in raisins. Spray an 8¼ × 4¼ × 3-inch loaf pan with nonstick vegetable cooking spray and pour batter in pan. Bake about 45 minutes *or* until toothpick inserted in center comes out clean. Cool in pan about 10 minutes. Remove from pan and cool completely on wire rack.

Makes 16 servings, 1 slice each.

Nutrients Per Serving:

165 Calories	22 grams Carbohydrates
3 grams Protein	35 milligrams Cholesterol
8 grams Fat	70 milligrams Sodium

BANANA NUT MUFFINS

¾ cup all-purpose flour
1¼ teaspoon baking powder
¼ teaspoon ground cinnamon
⅛ teaspoon baking soda
2 tablespoons solid vegetable shortening
¼ cup sugar
1 egg
2 small ripe bananas, mashed
20 whole almonds, chopped and toasted*

Preheat oven to 400°F. Spray 8 2½-inch muffin-pan cups with nonstick vegetable spray. In small bowl, with fork, mix flour, baking powder, cinnamon and baking soda. In large bowl, cream together shortening and sugar until fluffy. Beat in egg. Add flour mixture alternately with banana. Stir in almonds. Spoon batter into muffin-pan cups. Bake about 18–20 minutes until golden and toothpick inserted in center comes out clean. Immediately remove muffins from pan. Cool on wire rack.
Makes 4 servings, 2 muffins each.

*To toast almonds, spread almonds in single layer on a cookie sheet. Bake in 375°F oven about 5–10 minutes until just lightly browned, stirring occasionally.

Nutrients Per Serving:
295 Calories
6 grams Protein
12 grams Fat
43 grams Carbohydrates
70 milligrams Cholesterol
155 milligrams Sodium

VEGETABLE-STUFFED PITAS

1 cup small broccoli florets (about ¼ bunch)
½ cup small cauliflower florets (about ⅛ small head)
½ cup thinly sliced carrot (about 1 medium)
¼ cup chopped green pepper (about ¼ small)
¾ cup chopped tomato (about 1 large)
2 tablespoons chopped green onion (about 1 medium)
1 cup low-fat plain yogurt
2 tablespoons fresh lemon juice
1 garlic clove, minced
¾ teaspoon basil, crushed
¼ teaspoon oregano, crushed
⅛ teaspoon salt
⅛ teaspoon pepper
2 small whole-wheat pita bread pockets, halved
crosswise

In large saucepan over medium heat in 1 inch boiling water, heat broccoli, cauliflower, carrot and green pepper to boiling; cover and cook about 8–10 minutes until tender. Drain and cool. In large bowl, combine cooked vegetables, tomato and onion. In small bowl, combine remaining ingredients except pita bread pockets. Stir ½ cup of dressing into vegetables; toss well. Cover and chill 1 hour. Spoon an equal amount of vegetable mixture into each pita pocket half. Serve with remaining dressing.
Makes 4 servings.

Nutrients Per Serving:
105 Calories   20 grams Carbohydrates
  7 grams Protein   1 milligram Cholesterol
  1 gram Fat   135 milligrams Sodium

CRACKED WHEAT LONG JOHNS

½ cup skim milk, scalded
½ cup cracked bulgur wheat
3 tablespoons margarine, divided
2 tablespoons sugar
½ teaspoon salt
1 package active dry yeast
¾ cup lukewarm water (105°F–115°F)
1½ cups all-purpose flour
1¼ cups whole-wheat flour
¾ cup old-fashioned rolled oats

In small bowl, combine milk, cracked wheat, 2 tablespoons margarine, sugar and salt; cool to lukewarm. In large bowl, sprinkle yeast over warm water; set aside 5 minutes. With wooden spoon stir in milk mixture, 1¼ cups all-purpose flour, whole-wheat flour and oats to form soft dough. Turn dough onto lightly-floured surface and knead until smooth and elastic, about 10 minutes, adding additional all-purpose flour as necessary. Shape dough into a ball and place in a greased large bowl, turning over so that top of dough is greased. Cover with towel; let rise in a warm place until doubled in bulk, about 1 hour. Punch down dough. Turn dough onto lightly floured board; cut in half. With lightly-floured rolling pin, roll one-half of the dough into a 12-inch × 8-inch rectangle. Roll up dough jelly-roll fashion; pinch seam to seal and press ends to seal and tuck under. Place seam side down on greased baking sheet. Repeat with remaining portion of dough. Cover and let rise in a warm place until doubled in bulk, about 45 minutes. Preheat oven to 400°F. Melt remaining 1 tablespoon of the margarine; brush evenly over breads. Bake about 30 minutes, *or* until golden brown. Cool on wire racks.
Makes 12 servings, 2 loaves.

Nutrients Per Serving:
105 Calories   20 grams Carbohydrates
  7 grams Protein   0 milligrams Cholesterol
  1 gram Fat   130 milligrams Sodium

GREEK BREAD-BOX SANDWICH

1 6½-ounce can chunk white tuna in water, drained
  and flaked
⅓ cup low-fat plain yogurt
¼ cup diced red onion (about ¼ medium)
¼ cup diced green pepper (about ½ small)
1 ounce feta cheese, crumbled
¼ teaspoon dry mustard
½ teaspoon oregano, crushed
1 10-ounce loaf Italian whole-wheat bread

In medium bowl, combine all ingredients except bread. Cut top
quarter off bread; reserve. Remove inside, leaving ½-inch border
around bread; fill with tuna mixture. Replace top. Cut into 4 equal
pieces.
Makes 4 servings.

Nutrients Per Serving:
275 Calories   43 grams Carbohydrates
  19 grams Protein   30 milligrams Cholesterol
   3 grams Fat   670 milligrams Sodium

Desserts

OATMEAL SCONES

¼ cup nonfat dry milk
1 cup whole-wheat flour
½ cup all-purpose flour
1¼ cups uncooked oats
¼ cup sugar
1 tablespoon baking powder
¼ teaspoon ground cinnamon
½ cup margarine, melted
⅓ cup water
1 egg, beaten
½ cup raisins

Preheat oven to 425°F. In medium bowl, combine nonfat dry milk, flours, oats, sugar, baking powder, cream of tartar and cinnamon. Mix in margarine, water, egg and raisins. Shape dough into a ball and pat out lightly on a floured surface into an 8-inch circle. Turn onto greased baking sheet. Cut into 10 equal wedges. Bake for about 15 minutes until golden brown.
Makes 10 servings.

Nutrients Per Serving:

240 Calories   32 grams Carbohydrates
5 grams Protein   30 milligrams Cholesterol
11 grams Fat   245 milligrams Sodium

BAKED VANILLA CUSTARD

3 eggs, beaten
1½ cups skim milk, warm
2 tablespoons sugar
1 teaspoon vanilla
Dash nutmeg

Preheat oven to 325°F. Combine all ingredients except nutmeg. Pour into 1-quart baking dish. Sprinkle with nutmeg. Place in pan of warm water. Bake about 1 hour *or* until firm.
Makes 3 servings, about ¾ cup each.

Nutrients Per Serving:

160 Calories   15 grams Carbohydrates
10 grams Protein   275 milligrams Cholesterol
6 grams Fat   135 milligrams Sodium

BAKED ORANGE PUDDING

2 eggs, separated
⅛ teaspoon cream of tartar
⅔ cup skim milk
¼ cup orange juice
1 teaspoon honey
½ teaspoon grated orange peel
¼ cup all-purpose flour

Preheat oven to 300°F. In medium bowl with mixer at high speed, beat egg whites with cream of tartar until stiff peaks form; set aside. In medium bowl with mixer at high speed, beat egg yolks; beat in milk, orange juice, honey and orange peel. Add flour and beat until smooth. Fold mixture into egg whites. Spray a 1-quart baking dish with nonstick cooking spray and pour in mixture. Set dish in shallow baking pan; fill pan with 1–2 inches hot water. Bake about 35–40 minutes, until top springs back when touched. Serve hot *or* cold.
Makes 4 servings, ½ cup each.

Nutrients Per Serving:

95 Calories	12 grams Carbohydrates
5 grams Protein	140 milligrams Cholesterol
3 grams Fat	55 milligrams Sodium

BANANA TREATS

3 small bananas, cut into 1-inch sections
1 tablespoon honey
⅓ cup finely chopped unsalted peanuts

In medium bowl, toss banana sections and honey. Roll in finely chopped peanuts. Serve with toothpicks.
Makes 3 servings.

Nutrients Per Serving:

165 Calories	29 grams Carbohydrates
3 grams Protein	0 milligrams Cholesterol
5 grams Fat	2 milligrams Sodium

BLUEBERRY YOGURT CREAM PIE

1½ cups vanilla wafer crumbs
4 tablespoons margarine
¾ cup and 2 tablespoons water
1 envelope unflavored gelatin
1½ cups part-skim ricotta cheese (about 12 ounces)
4 tablespoons sugar, divided
1½ cups low-fat lemon yogurt
⅛ teaspoon ground nutmeg
1 cup unsweetened frozen blueberries
1 tablespoon cornstarch
½ teaspoon fresh lemon juice

Preheat oven to 375°F. In small bowl, combine vanilla wafer crumbs and margarine. With back of spoon, press mixture into bottom and sides of a 9-inch pie plate, making a small rim. Bake 8 minutes; cool on wire rack. In small saucepan, combine ¼ cup of the water and gelatin; set aside about 5 minutes to soften. Cook over low heat until gelatin dissolves. In medium bowl, with electric mixer on medium speed, cream ricotta cheese and 2 tablespoons sugar until fluffy. Stir in yogurt and nutmeg; mix well. Stir in gelatin mixture. Spread into pie crust; chill about 1 hour. Meanwhile, in small saucepan, heat blueberries, ½ cup water, and remaining 2 tablespoons sugar to boiling. Combine 2 tablespoons water, cornstarch and lemon juice. Stir into blueberries and cook about 30 seconds until thick, stirring constantly. Cool to room temperature. Spread evenly over crust. Chill until pie is firm, about 2 hours.
Makes 10 servings.

Nutrients Per Serving:
215 Calories
8 grams Protein
10 grams Fat
24 grams Carbohydrates
20 milligrams Cholesterol
165 milligrams Sodium

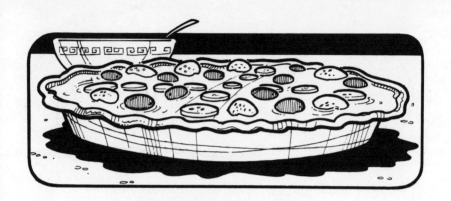

FRESH FRUIT FLAN

1¼ cups graham cracker crumbs (16 crackers)
3 tablespoons margarine, melted
5 tablespoons cornstarch, divided
¼ cup sugar
2 cups skim milk
2 egg yolks, beaten
1 teaspoon vanilla extract
½ teaspoon coconut extract
1 8-ounce can pineapple chunks in juice, drained, reserve juice
1½ cups sliced strawberries (about 1 pint)
½ small banana, sliced
12 green grapes

Preheat oven to 375°F. In small bowl, combine graham cracker crumbs and margarine. With back of spoon, press mixture into bottom and sides of a 9-inch pie plate, making small rim. Bake 8 minutes; cool on wire rack. In medium saucepan, combine 4 tablespoons of cornstarch and sugar. Gradually add milk, stirring to blend. Bring to boil over medium-high heat, stirring constantly. Mix about ½ cup hot mixture into egg yolks. Return mixture to pan and cook about 2 minutes, stirring constantly. Stir in vanilla and coconut extract. Cool to room temperature. Spread custard over bottom of pie shell. Arrange fruits over custard. Add enough water to pineapple juice to make ¾ cup. Stir in remaining 1 tablespoon cornstarch. Heat over low heat until thickened and clear; cool slightly and spoon evenly over fruit.
Makes 8 servings.

Nutrients Per Serving:
210 Calories
4 grams Protein
7 grams Fat
33 grams Carbohydrates
70 milligrams Cholesterol
180 milligrams Sodium

FRUIT-FILLED "CREAM" PUFF RING

½ cup all-purpose flour
½ cup whole-wheat flour
1 cup water
4 tablespoons margarine
4 eggs
1½ cups sliced strawberries (about ¾ pint)
2 medium peaches, sliced
½ small banana, sliced
12 green grapes
½ cup orange-flavored liqueur

Preheat oven to 375°F. In small bowl, combine flours. Spray baking sheet with nonstick vegetable cooking spray. In medium saucepan over high heat, heat water and margarine to boiling. Reduce heat to low; with wooden spoon, vigorously stir in flours until mixture forms ball and leaves side of pan; remove from heat. Add eggs, one at a time, beating well after each addition, until smooth. Drop batter on a baking sheet in mounded tablespoonfuls, touching each other, to form a 6-inch circle. Bake about 45 minutes *or* until puffy and golden brown. Cut off top of each puff and reserve; remove and discard soft dough in center. Cool on wire rack. Meanwhile, in large bowl, combine fruits. Pour liqueur over fruit; toss to coat well. Cover and refrigerate about 2 hours, stirring occasionally. Drain fruit reserving liquid. Spoon fruit into each cream puff. Replace tops. Serve with reserved liquid.
Makes 12 servings.

Nutrients Per Serving:

145 Calories	16 grams Carbohydrates
4 grams Protein	90 milligrams Cholesterol
6 grams Fat	70 milligrams Sodium

LEMON BAVARIAN CRÈME

2 cups skim milk
1 envelope unflavored gelatin
½ teaspoon vanilla
2 egg yolks, beaten
½ cup part-skim ricotta cheese (about 4 ounces)
⅓ cup honey
1 teaspoon grated lemon peel
Juice of one lemon
4 egg whites
Lemon slices (to decorate)

In medium saucepan, heat milk, gelatin and vanilla, stirring constantly until gelatin dissolves. Slowly stir half of gelatin mixture
into egg yolks, then pour yolk mixture into saucepan. Heat until
mixture coats a metal spoon (which happens almost immediately).
Place saucepan into bowl of ice water and stir until cool. Pour
cooled mixture into blender and add ricotta and honey; process
until smooth. Stir in lemon peel and juice; pour mixture into
medium bowl. Refrigerate and chill until thick enough to mound
from a spoon, approximately ½ hour. In small bowl, beat egg
whites until slightly peaked. Stir one-half of egg whites into custard. Then carefully fold in remaining egg whites. Turn into a 1½-
quart mold lined with lemon slices and chill at least 4 hours.
Makes 8 servings, ¾ cup each.

Nutrients Per Serving:

115 Calories	16 grams Carbohydrates
7 grams Protein	75 milligrams Cholesterol
3 grams Fat	80 milligrams Sodium

MINTED ORANGE LEMON ICE

3 cups orange juice
1 cup fresh lemon juice
2 teaspoons dried mint leaves
1 envelope unflavored gelatin
3 tablespoons sugar
2 egg whites

In medium saucepan over low heat, simmer orange juice, lemon juice and mint leaves, covered, about 10 minutes. Let cool to room temperature. Strain juice and discard mint. In medium saucepan, combine gelatin and sugar. Gradually add juice. Heat over low heat until sugar and gelatin dissolve. Pour into shallow metal pan. Freeze until partially frozen, about 2 hours. Spoon mixture into a large bowl; beat with electric mixer on medium speed until slushy. In small bowl, beat egg whites until soft peaks form. Fold into fruit mixture. Freeze until firm, about 3 hours. Let ice stand at room temperature 10 minutes before serving.
Makes 6 servings, about ¾ cup each.

Nutrients Per Serving:

100 Calories   23 grams Carbohydrates
  3 grams Protein   0 milligrams Cholesterol
  trace of Fat   20 milligrams Sodium

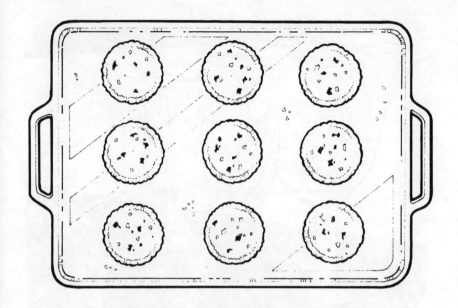

PEANUT BUTTER RAISIN COOKIES

1¼ cups all-purpose flour
½ teaspoon baking powder
¼ teaspoon ground cinnamon
⅛ teaspoon ground cloves
4 tablespoons margarine, softened
½ cup firmly-packed light brown sugar
1 egg
½ cup crunchy peanut butter
2 tablespoons skim milk
6 tablespoons raisins

Preheat oven to 375°F. Spray 2 baking sheets with nonstick vegetable cooking spray. In small bowl, combine flour, baking powder and spices; set aside. In large bowl, with mixer on medium speed, cream margarine and brown sugar until light and fluffy. Beat in egg until well blended. Beat in peanut butter and milk until smooth. Beat in reserved dry ingredients until just blended. Stir in raisins. Drop dough by teaspoonfuls, about 2 inches apart on to baking sheets. Bake 10 minutes until golden. Cool on wire racks. Makes 3 dozen cookies, 3 cookies per serving.

Nutrients Per Serving:
200 Calories   25 grams Carbohydrates
  5 grams Protein   25 milligrams Cholesterol
 10 grams Fat   135 milligrams Sodium

MOCHA-FILLED "CREAM" PUFFS

½ cup water
2 tablespoons margarine
½ cup all-purpose flour
2 eggs
1 tablespoon skim milk
1 tablespoon unsweetened cocoa
1 teaspoon instant coffee powder
¾ cup part-skim ricotta cheese (about 6 ounces)
3 tablespoons sugar
¼ cup low-fat plain yogurt
1 teaspoon vanilla extract

Preheat oven to 375°F. Spray baking sheet with nonstick vegetable cooking spray. In small saucepan over high heat, heat water and margarine to boiling. Reduce heat to low; with wooden spoon vigorously stir in flour until mixture forms ball and leaves side of pan; remove from heat. Add eggs, one at a time, beating well after each addition, until smooth. Drop batter on baking sheet in 6 large mounds, 3 inches apart. Bake about 30 minutes *or* until puffy and golden brown. Cut off tops and reserve; remove and discard soft dough in center. Cool on wire racks. In small bowl, combine milk, cocoa and coffee powder until cocoa and coffee dissolve. In medium bowl, cream together ricotta cheese and sugar until fluffy. Beat in chocolate mixture, yogurt and vanilla until smooth. Spoon into each cream puff, replace tops.
Makes 6 servings.

Nutrients Per Serving:
180 Calories   20 grams Carbohydrates
  8 grams Protein   100 milligrams Cholesterol
  8 grams Fat   115 milligrams Sodium

PINEAPPLE MERINGUE PIE

1¼ cups all-purpose flour
5 tablespoons solid vegetable shortening
4–5 tablespoons ice water
1 8-ounce can crushed pineapple, in juice, drained,
  reserve juice
1⅓ cups unsweetened pineapple juice
½ cup cornstarch
6 tablespoons sugar, divided
½ teaspoon grated orange peel
4 eggs, separated
1 tablespoon magarine
¼ teaspoon cream of tartar

Preheat oven to 425°F. Place flour in medium bowl. With pastry blender or 2 knives used scissor fashion, cut shortening into flour until mixture resembles coarse crumbs. Sprinkle water, 1 tablespoon at a time, into flour mixture, mixing with a fork until pastry is moist enough to hold together. Shape pastry into a ball. On a lightly floured surface, with lightly floured rolling pin, roll pastry into circle, about 2 inches larger than a 9-inch pie plate. Fit pastry into pie plate. Trim edges, leaving a 1-inch overhang. Fold overhang under, forming a rim; flute edge. Prick bottom and sides of pie crust with a fork. Bake 20 minutes until golden. Cool completely on wire rack. Reduce oven temperature to 400°F. Add pineapple juice to reserved juice. In medium saucepan, combine cornstarch and 4 tablespoons of the sugar. Stir in pineapple juice. Cook over medium heat, stirring constantly, until mixture is thickened and smooth. Stir in orange peel; cook about 2 minutes, stirring constantly. Beat egg yolks. Stir about ½ cup hot mixture into egg yolks. Return mixture to saucepan; cook, stirring vigorously, over low heat, about 2 minutes. Do not boil. Stir in crushed pineapple and margarine. Pour into piecrust. In small bowl, with mixer at high speed, beat egg whites with cream of tartar until soft peaks form. Beating at high speed, gradually add remaining 2 tablespoons sugar, beating until stiff peaks form. Spread meringue over filling, sealing edges. Bake about 8–10 minutes until lightly browned. Cool, then refrigerate.
Makes 10 servings.

Nutrients Per Serving:

240 Calories	33 grams Carbohydrates
4 grams Protein	110 milligrams Cholesterol
10 grams Fat	40 milligrams Sodium

SPICED POACHED PEARS

4 small pears, peeled
1 cup water
½ cup dry port wine
1 cinnamon stick
½ teaspoon whole cloves
½ teaspoon grated lemon peel

Starting from bottom of pears, remove cores, being careful not to go all the way through top. In medium saucepan, heat water, wine, spices and lemon peel to boiling. Reduce heat to low; cover and simmer about 10 minutes. Add pears and simmer, covered, about 30 minutes longer until tender. Pour into large bowl. Cover and let stand at room temperature 2 hours. Remove and discard spices. Serve pears with cooking liquid.
Makes 4 servings.

Nutrients Per Serving:

135 Calories	26 grams Carbohydrates
1 gram Protein	0 milligrams Cholesterol
1 gram Fat	1 milligram Sodium

STRAWBERRY WAFFLES WITH COGNAC

1½ cups strawberries
2 tablespoons cognac
½ teaspoon vanilla extract
4 frozen waffles, toasted
2 cups vanilla ice milk
2 small bananas, sliced

In covered blender at medium speed, puree one-half of the strawberries; pour into small bowl. Repeat with remaining strawberries. Stir in cognac and vanilla extract. Cover and refrigerate about 2 hours. On each waffle, spoon ½ cup ice milk. Garnish each waffle with an equal amount of bananas. Spoon strawberry sauce over top of each dessert.
Makes 4 servings.

Nutrients Per Serving:

265 Calories	44 grams Carbohydrates
6 grams Protein	40 milligrams Cholesterol
6 grams Fat	215 milligrams Sodium

PEACH BREAD PUDDING

6 slices day-old or stale bread
8 dates, chopped (about 2⅓ ounces)
2 medium peaches, peeled and sliced (about 9 ounces)
2½ cups skim milk
3 eggs, beaten
4 tablespoons sugar
¼ teaspoon ground cinnamon
⅛ teaspoon ground nutmeg

Spray 1½-quart casserole with nonstick cooking spray. Cut each bread slice into quarters. Layer one half of bread pieces on bottom of casserole; sprinkle with one-half of the dates and one-half of the peaches. Top with remaining bread and fruits. In medium bowl with electric mixer, beat milk, eggs, sugar and spices until well mixed; pour over bread. Let stand at room temperature about 1 hour. Preheat oven to 350°F. Set casserole in larger, deep baking dish; place on oven rack. Fill dish with hot water to a depth of 1 inch. Bake about 50 to 60 minutes or until knife inserted in center comes out clean. Serve warm.
Makes 6 servings, 1 cup each.

Nutrients Per Serving:
220 Calories   38 grams Carbohydrates
   9 grams Protein   140 milligrams Cholesterol
   4 grams Fat   205 milligrams Sodium

STRAWBERRY PARFAIT

1 cup regular long-grain rice
2 cups skim milk
3 tablespoons cornstarch
3 tablespoons sugar
½ teaspoon grated lemon rind
¼ teaspoon ground cinnamon
⅛ teaspoon ground nutmeg
1 egg, beaten
1 teaspoon vanilla extract
2 cups sliced fresh strawberries

Prepare rice as label directs, omitting salt and butter; cool slightly. In medium saucepan, combine milk, cornstarch, sugar, lemon rind, cinnamon and nutmeg; bring to a boil, stirring constantly. Pour a small amount of hot mixture into egg, stirring constantly. Return mixture to saucepan; cook and stir over low heat until slightly thickened. Stir in cooked rice and vanilla. Pour into bowl. Cover and refrigerate until chilled, about 3 hours. In each of 4 parfait glasses, layer ¼ cup rice mixture and 2 rounded tablespoons strawberries. Repeat layers of rice mixture and strawberries, ending with strawberries.
Makes 4 servings, about 1½ cups each.

Nutrients Per Serving:
325 Calories
9 grams Protein
2 grams Fat
65 grams Carbohydrates
70 milligrams Cholesterol
85 milligrams Sodium

STRAWBERRY YOGURT POPS

20 ounces frozen unsweetened strawberries, thawed,
   drained, reserving liquid
1 envelope unflavored gelatin
2 cups low-fat plain yogurt
12 3-ounce paper cups
12 wooden sticks

In small saucepan, add reserved liquid and sprinkle with gelatin.
Cook over low heat, stirring constantly·until gelatin dissolves. Mix
strawberries, yogurt and gelatin mixture in blender until smooth.
Fill cups with mixture and cover with foil. Insert sticks through foil
into mixture so that foil holds sticks in place. Freeze until solid. To
unmold, dip cup into warm water and slip off cup.
Makes 12 servings.

Nutrients Per Serving:

40 Calories	7 grams Carbohydrates
3 grams Protein	1 milligram Cholesterol
trace of Fat	30 milligrams Sodium

Beverages

APPLEBERRY SPRITZER

1½ cups whole strawberries
⅔ cup apple juice
½ cup club soda

Set aside 2 whole strawberries for garnish. In blender container at medium speed, process remaining strawberries and apple juice until smooth. Add club soda. Pour into 2 glasses. Garnish each glass with reserved strawberries.
Makes 2 servings.

Nutrients Per Serving:

75 Calories	18 grams Carbohydrates
1 gram Protein	0 milligrams Cholesterol
1 gram Fat	5 milligrams Sodium

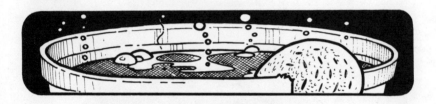

SPICED CRANORANGE PUNCH

3 cups low-calorie cranberry juice cocktail
1 cup orange juice
2 cinnamon sticks
½ teaspoon whole cloves
1 cup seltzer
Ice cubes
Orange slices

In medium saucepan over medium heat, heat cranberry juice, orange juice, cinnamon sticks and cloves to boiling. Reduce heat to low; cover and simmer about 15 minutes until flavor develops. Strain juice into a punch bowl *or* large pitcher. Cover and chill about 2 hours. Just before serving, add seltzer, ice cubes and orange slices.
Makes 8 servings, ⅔ cup each.

Nutrients Per Serving:

30 Calories	8 grams Carbohydrates
trace of Protein	0 milligrams Cholesterol
trace of Fat	5 milligrams Sodium

PINEAPPLE SLUSH

2 cups crushed ice
1 8-ounce can crushed pineapple in its own juice
⅓ cup unsweetened pineapple juice

In blender at medium speed, process one-half of all ingredients to slushy consistency. Pour into glass. Repeat with remaining ingredients.
Makes 2 servings.

Nutrients Per Serving:

90 Calories	23 grams Carbohydrates
1 gram Protein	0 milligrams Cholesterol
trace of Fat	trace of Sodium

CAPPUCCINO MILK SHAKE

1 cup skim milk
½ cup chocolate ice milk
1½ teaspoons instant coffee powder
⅛ teaspoon ground cinnamon

In blender at low speed, process all ingredients until smooth.
Makes 1 serving.

Nutrients Per Serving:

220 Calories	33 grams Carbohydrates
12 grams Protein	20 milligrams Cholesterol
4 grams Fat	205 milligrams Sodium

AFTER DINNER CAFÉ

2 cups hot coffee
1 small piece lemon peel
1 whole cinnamon stick
2 tablespoons coffee-flavored liqueur

In small saucepan over low heat, heat coffee, lemon peel and cinnamon stick, covered, about 7 minutes. Stir in liqueur. Remove and discard lemon peel.
Makes 2 servings.

Nutrients Per Serving:

45 Calories	5 grams Carbohydrates
trace of Protein	0 milligrams Cholesterol
trace of Fat	2 milligrams Sodium

HOT MULLED WINE

3 cups apple juice
6 cinnamon sticks
1 teaspoon whole cloves
6 thin lemon slices
1 large orange, sliced
3 cups dry red wine

In medium saucepan over medium-high heat, combine all ingredients except wine. Bring to boil and boil about 5 minutes. Add wine and bring to a boil again. Remove from heat. Serve hot or chilled over ice.
Makes 12 servings, ½ cup each.

Nutrients Per Serving:

90 Calories	13 grams Carbohydrates
trace of Protein	0 milligrams Cholesterol
trace of Fat	5 milligrams Sodium

COCO-BANANA MILK SHAKE

1 cup skim milk
½ small banana
½ teaspoon vanilla extract
¼ teaspoon coconut extract

In blender container at low speed, process all ingredients until smooth.
Makes 1 serving.

Nutrients Per Serving:

140 Calories   23 grams Carbohydrates
  9 grams Protein   5 milligrams Cholesterol
  1 gram Fat   130 milligrams Sodium

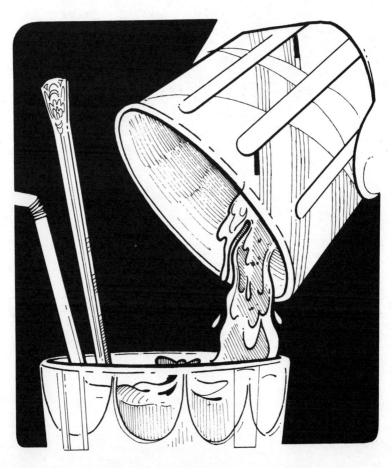

VII
Food Shopping, Storing and Preparation

This chapter will show you how to make educated food choices in the supermarket, how to store foods to maintain nutritional quality and safety, and how to modify your own recipes the *Eat Well, Be Well®* way.

In the Supermarket

What's in the Food You Buy?

Which foods should you choose? First, be familiar with food labels. They can provide a wealth of information about the content of food. And they can help you decide which products best suit your needs.

Label Reading

Basic Information

The federal Food and Drug Administration (FDA) requires that certain information be on all food labels. This includes:

The name of the product.

Total or net contents or weight, including the liquid in which the product is packed.

Name and address of manufacturer, packer or distributor.

List of ingredients. Ingredients are listed in descending order by weight. Thus, the first ingredient on the label is present in the largest amount, the second ingredient is the second largest amount and so forth. Only labels for "standardized" foods need not list ingredients. Such foods are made according to formulas set by the FDA. You can find out the ingredients of standardized foods by writing the manufacturer or the FDA.

Nutrition Information

If a label or advertisement makes any nutritional claim about the product, then nutrition information must be given on the label. Thus, if an ad for a drink boasts "more vitamin C than fresh orange juice," the label for that drink must specify the amount of vitamin C it contains. The label of "enriched" or "fortified" products must also provide verifying data.

Nutrition labels include the following information:

Serving (portion) size: the amount of food for which nutrition information is given, such as two slices, one-half cup, three ounces.

The number of calories and grams of fat, protein and carbohydrate contained in one serving.

The percentage of U.S. Recommended Dietary Allowances of protein and seven vitamins and minerals in one serving of the product.

Nutritional information such as cholesterol, saturated and polyunsaturated fat and sodium contents must be included if a nutritional claim has been made, such as "low-sodium product" or "polyunsaturated."

Other information that you might find on a label includes freshness dates, grades of quality such as Grade A or Prime, and codes or symbols for a store's inventory control.

Once you understand how a label is set up, you can familiarize yourself with the ingredients you find listed. This is especially important if you are concerned with moderating your intake of sodium, fat and sugar. If you are on a strict diet prescribed by your doctor for health reasons, label reading is essential.

Sodium

First, let's take a look at the sodium content of certain foods. Keep in mind that sodium is part of many compounds; it's not only salt (sodium chloride) that you need to watch out for. You also need to be alert to: monosodium glutamate (MSG), sodium silicoaluminate, sodium sulfite, sodium bisulfite, sodium phosphate. Other sodium containing ingredients to look for on labels include sodium citrate, sodium saccharin, sodium benzoate, baking soda (sodium bicarbonate), baking powder and brine.

It's important to remember that sodium compounds such as these may not taste salty and often other ingredients will mask the taste of common table salt, so don't rely on your taste buds. In many cases, you can't know whether a product is high in sodium unless you read the label.

Surprisingly, the sodium content of many foods such as most breakfast cereals, packaged puddings and cake mixes, cooking wines and sherries, club soda, cheese, buttermilk, commercially prepared baked goods, canned foods and frozen entrees is often quite high, although they may not taste salty.

Sugar

Sugar, like sodium, is added to food in a variety of forms. Besides obviously sweet foods such as jams, jellies, soft drinks, pies and cakes, many other commercially prepared foods contain substantial amounts of sugar without actually tasting sweet. Tomato sauce and catsup, salad dressings and peanut butter are prime examples.

To spot this hidden sugar, you have to be aware that there are numerous types of sweeteners, often listed separately. Look for these words on the label: sucrose, glucose, dextrose, fructose, lactose, maltose, corn syrups, corn sweeteners, honey, molasses, levulose, invert sugar, turbinado sugar and brown sugar. These ingredients are all sugars and make up the total amount of sugar contained in a product.

Fat

If you are concerned about the amount or type of fat in your diet, label reading can help you make smart choices. Saturated fats that are often added to foods include: lard, suet, butter, coconut oil, cream, hydrogenated fat or oil, cocoa butter, palm or palm kernel oil, shortening and bacon, beef or chicken fat.

What Do These Words Really Mean?

"Sugar free," "lite," "reduced calorie," "sodium reduced," "imitation." The choices for a shopper on a restricted diet are no longer few and far between. But having such a wide and growing selection of products to choose from won't help unless you know what you're really buying. Here are some terms and explanations of what they mean:

"Low Calorie"

By law, a food labeled "low calorie" must contain no more than 40 calories per serving and contain 0.4 calories or less per gram (11.36 calories or less per ounce).

"Reduced Calorie"

A food that contains too many calories to be labeled low calorie can be labeled "reduced calorie" if it contains at least one-third fewer calories than a similar food in which calories are not reduced. Thus, salad dressings, which contain too many calories per gram to be labeled "low calorie," are usually labeled "reduced calorie."

The label of a reduced-calorie food must also compare its calorie content with an unmodified version of the product, such as: "Reduced-calorie blue cheese dressing, 45 calories per serving; regular blue cheese dressing, 80 calories per serving."

"Lite" or "Light"

There is no legal definition for these terms, so you must read the label carefully to see what you are getting. While most of the new lighter foods contain less of such substances as fat, sugar or alcohol (in the case of wine or beer) and hence, fewer calories, there are no guarantees unless the products are labeled "low calorie" or "reduced calorie."

"Sugar Free" or "Sugarless"

A product that is sugar free or sugarless, is not necessarily low or reduced in calories. For instance, a sugar-free chocolate bar may contain sorbitol, a sweetener with a caloric value similar to sugar. If this is the case, the label must indicate in some way that the product isn't for weight control. Read carefully! Many sugar-free chewing gums contain calories but their sweetener does not promote tooth decay.

"Diabetic"

A food that is marketed specifically for people with diabetes must state on its label: "Diabetics: This product may be useful in your diet on the advice of a physician." If the food is not reduced calorie (many contain even more calories than the usual variety), the label must specify, "This food is not a reduced-calorie food."

"Imitation"

If a food is labeled as an "imitation" of another food, it means that the substitute product is not as nutritious as the product it resembles. Thus, an imitation cheese provides fewer nutrients per serving than real cheese, which has a legal standard of identity. If you are following a special diet, certain imitation products may have benefits that are important to you such as reduced-sodium, -calorie or -cholesterol content. A careful study of the label can tell you if the imitation product is for you or if you should stick to the real thing.

"Dietetic"

A food item can be labeled "diet" or "dietetic" only if it meets the requirements for a low- or reduced-calorie food, or if it is clearly intended for a special dietary purpose other than weight control, such as "for low-sodium diets." Again, the label should tell the tale.

Is "Natural" Better?

Just because a product label says it's "natural" doesn't mean it is any better for you than the same product that is not labeled as natural. Potato chips, for example, may sport an "all natural" label because they contain sea salt and no additives, but they are still high in sodium and may also be high in fat and calories.

If you look closely at the ingredients, you'll often find that the word natural refers to only a single natural ingredient in an otherwise artificial product such as a beverage containing water, sugar, artificial coloring and *natural* lemon flavor.

Some of these foods labeled "natural" cost more, but don't think that they all provide better nutritional quality or safety than conventional foods. Before you pay a higher price for a "natural" food, read the ingredients carefully to be sure you are getting your money's worth.

What About Food Additives?

Food additives, whether natural or synthetic, serve to make our food supply more nutritious, longer lasting, less expensive and better tasting. But the large number of additives and their "chemical sounding" names cause much confusion on the part of the consumer.

Actually, additives make up less than one percent of our food. And sugar, salt, corn sweetener, citric acid (found naturally in oranges and lemons), baking soda, vegetable colors, mustard and pepper account for 98 percent by weight of all food additives used in the United States.

Many additives sound like chemicals, because they are. But *all* foods are mixtures of chemicals whether the chemicals are natural or synthetic. Many of the chemicals produced synthetically and added to food are the same chemicals that occur naturally in food. For example, there is enough of the preservative calcium propionate *naturally* present in an ounce of Swiss cheese to preserve two pounds of white bread.

Despite misplaced nostalgia for the good old days when food was "wholesome," the food additives used today are more strictly regulated than at any other time in history. At the turn of the century, manufacturers freely used pigments containing toxic metals such as lead, copper and arsenic as coloring agents and stretched pepper with bits of charcoal.

If you are concerned about food additives, read labels to find out what is in the food you buy. Then learn what the various additives do and decide which ones are of concern to you. Once you are informed, you can select food on the basis of which characteristics—convenience, taste, eye appeal, cost, storage time—mean the most to you. Ultimately the choice is yours.

In Your Kitchen

Cooking the *Eat Well, Be Well*® Way

You're going to enjoy the *Eat Well, Be Well*® recipes and some will become regulars in your menu plans. But, you'll undoubtedly want to continue using many of your old favorite recipes, too. Using the *Eat Well, Be Well*® cooking techniques, you can reduce the sodium, sugar, cholesterol, fat and calories in many of your traditional favorites. Here are some hints for modifying recipes to follow the Dietary Guidelines:

Consider changing the cooking methods used in the recipe. The nutritional content for a given item can vary greatly, depending on how it is prepared. Often you can slash calories and fat by using a cooking method different from the one called for in the recipe. Some examples: brown pot roast or stew meat under the broiler instead of in fat or oil; try oven frying instead of deep-fat frying; steam vegetables in a little liquid instead of sautéing them in oil.

Add calorie-saving techniques the recipe doesn't mention. This can be as simple as removing the skin from chicken or trimming the fat from the meat before cooking. Get in the habit of draining, skimming or blotting excess fat from everything possible when you're cooking, even if the recipe doesn't mention it.

Skip steps that add calories if they aren't essential to the taste of the product. Don't flour meat pieces before you brown them. Use nonstick cookware or nonstick vegetable cooking sprays and ignore instructions to butter casseroles and baking pans. Forget sautéing vegetables in oil if you are going to add them to a long-cooking sauce or stew. The vegetables will cook while the sauce or stew simmers.

Check to see if you can completely eliminate high-fat, high-calorie, high-sodium ingredients. It's easy enough to omit butter, margarine and salt often included in recipes for rice, pasta and vegetables, and you'll never miss them if you plan to add a sauce or other seasonings. If sodium is a problem, skip such garnishes as capers, olives and anchovies. Dishes seldom need added salt when the recipe calls for high-salt items like bouillon cubes, soy sauce, many canned products or salt-containing seasonings.

If you can't eliminate high-calorie, high-sodium, or high-fat ingredients, analyze the recipe to see if you can reduce them. Experiment. Some sugar is needed in cakes, cookies and quick breads, but you can often reduce the amounts by one-third or more and still get an acceptable result. Try cutting the amount of salt in the recipe in half. Always use the minimum amount of oil necessary to brown or sauté regardless of what the recipe calls for. Use less meat in casseroles or stews and extend the dish with vegetables and or grains (pasta, rice, etc.) to get the same number of servings but less fat, less cholesterol and fewer calories.

Try to substitute high-fat, high-calorie and high-sodium ingredients with more acceptable products. Use lean cuts of meat when the recipe calls for fatty cuts. Experiment with cholesterol-free tofu in dishes such as chili, spaghetti sauce, casseroles. Use wine or homemade stock instead of salty canned broths and bouillon cubes, and substitute herbs, spices, pepper, lemon and vinegar for salt when possible. Look at the calories you can save by making the following simple substitutions:

Instead of	Calories	Use	Calories	Save
1 cup whole milk	150	1 cup skim milk	90	60
1 cup sour cream	495	1 cup plain low-fat yogurt	145	350
1 cup heavy cream	820	1 cup evaporated skim milk	200	620
1 cup creamed cottage cheese (4% fat)	235	1 cup low-fat cottage cheese	165	70
1 ounce cream cheese	100	1 ounce Neufchatel cheese	70	30
3½-oz. roast duck	337	3½ oz. roast chicken breast	222	115
4 oz. ground beef	224	4 oz. extra lean ground beef	140	84
6½-oz. can oil-packed tuna	530	6½-oz. can water-packed tuna	234	296

Read "The Dieter's Guide to Calorie Cutting" (page 66) to get ideas for low-calorie techniques and substitutes that may be useful in your recipes. Soon cooking the *Eat Well, Be Well*® way will become routine. You may also be surprised to discover that you prefer the new "light" taste of traditional favorites.

Tips for a Healthy Budget, Too

Practice Good Nutrition

Today's costs make everyone take a second look at the food they're buying. Shoppers want to keep their budget in line, but they also want to get the most nutrition for their money.

Following the *Eat Well, Be Well*® diet plan shouldn't cost you more than you are spending now, and it could actually reduce your food costs. Foods claiming the biggest chunk of your food dollar are often those highest in fat, cholesterol and calories: prime grades of highly marbled meats, butter, cream, cheeses and rich desserts. On the other hand, legumes, fruits and vegetables in season, grains, smaller portions of lean cuts of meat, many varieties of fish and chicken are more economical. Convenience and snack foods often have high prices in relation to the nutrients they provide, and many of these items are high in sugar, fat and/or sodium.

Plan Ahead

Take the time to plan your meals, using the Basic Four Food Groups as a guide. It's worth the effort. You'll find it easier to stay with your food plan if you know beforehand what your next meal will be. Planning ahead can also help you shop wisely, taking advantage of store specials to save money.

Center your menus around in-season foods so that you don't get stuck paying out-of-season prices. Be creative with unsweetened canned and frozen fruits and vegetables when the prices of fresh fruits and vegetables are too high.

Smart Shopping

When you're at the store, follow your grocery list closely. Avoid impulse buying of unneeded items, but remain flexible so you can take advantage of unadvertised specials. Substitute one food for another when your planned choice is unavailable or the price is too high.

Use unit pricing, when available, to help you choose from various brands and sizes. Store brands are often a better buy unless you have a refund or cents-off coupon, and generic or no-name brands are often even better bargains because costly advertising and packaging have been eliminated. But generic brands tend to be lower in quality in terms of appearance or uniformity, even though they are equally nutritious, so consider how you plan to use the item before making your choice.

Buying foods in quantity can save you money, but only if you have the space to store the extra properly and if it is an item that you use regularly. Nothing keeps forever without losing quality and nutrients. Herbs, spices, grains and flours are often much less expensive when bought in bulk. If you can't use the larger amounts yourself, consider buying them with a neighbor.

Many food products, particularly perishables, carry dates to which the manufacturer guarantees product quality and freshness. However, those dates can mean different things on different types of food. For example, a "pack" date indicates the day a product was manufactured, processed or packaged. A "pull" or "sell" date recommends the last day of sale that allows sufficient time for home storage and use. A "freshness" date is the date after which a product is not likely to be at peak quality. And an "expiration" date is the last date after which quality of a product is no longer assured.

Food Storage

Regardless of how fresh a food is when you buy it, if you don't handle and store it properly, it can lose both quality and nutrient value. Here are some guidelines to protect your investment:

Store canned and packaged dry foods in a cool, dry place—not over the stove where high temperatures can cause nutrient loss. Length of storage time is also an important factor in nutrient content, so first use those foods stored longest.

Foods that require refrigeration need more careful handling. Keep your refrigerator temperatures between 34° to 40°F and store the foods without crowding, allowing air to circulate freely between them.

Loosely wrap fresh meats and poultry in wax paper or aluminum foil and store in the meat compartment or the coldest part of your refrigerator. Again, allow sufficient space between packages for air circulation.

Dairy products such as eggs, milk, cream, cottage and ricotta cheese, yogurt, butter and similar products should remain in their original containers. Be sure to reclose them tightly, however. These foods easily pick up odors from other foods in the refrigerator.

Store most fresh vegetables and ripe fruits, dry and unwashed, in the refrigerator. But do not refrigerate potatoes, onions and beets; store them in a cool dry place. Tomato growers warn that refrigeration destroys the flavor of fresh tomatoes.

Check your freezer temperature. Frozen food should be stored at a temperature of 0°F; store only small quantities of frozen food; u and replenish your supply frequently.

The following chart gives optimum storage periods for various foods.

Refrigerator and Freezer Storage Periods

Food	Refrigerator	Freezer
Cheese		
hard	4–8 weeks	6 months
soft	1–2 weeks	not recommended
Milk	1 week	3 months
Cream (ultra-pasteurized)	4 weeks	4 months
Eggs	2–3 weeks	9 months
Meat		
Bacon	5–7 days	1 month
Beef		
whole cuts	2–4 days	6–12 months
ground	1–2 days	3–4 months
Frankfurters	4–5 days	1 month
Ham	3–4 days	2 months
Lamb	2–4 days	6–9 months
Luncheon Meats	1 week	not recommended
Pork	2–4 days	3–6 months
Sausage	1 week	1–2 months
Veal	2–4 days	6–9 months

Food	Refrigerator	Freezer
Leftover Cooked Meats	4–5 days	*
Leftover Casseroles, Main Dishes, Soups	2–3 days	*
Poultry		
Chicken	1–2 days	12 months
Game Birds	1–2 days	8–12 months
Turkey, Duck, Goose	1–2 days	6–8 months
Fish		
Lean (Trout, Haddock, Salmon)	1–2 days	6–8 months
Fat (Scallops, Halibut, Whitefish)	1–2 days	3–4 months
Shellfish	1–2 days	4–6 months
Fruits		
fresh	1–2 weeks	9–12 months**
canned	3–5 days***	9–12 months
Vegetables		
fresh	1–14 days	9–12 months**
canned	3 days***	9–12 months
Baked Goods		
Pies, Pastry	4–6 days	6 months
Baked Quickbreads	4–7 days	3 months
Cookies, Cakes	3 days	2 months
Cake Batter	not recommended	1 week
Cookie Dough	not recommended	9–12 months
Yeast Breads, Rolls	7–14 days	6–9 months
Flour	12 months	12 months

---

* Depends on ingredients.
** Except for lemons and limes, which do not freeze well.
*** Always remove contents from can after opening it and store in glass jar or plastic container.

Appendix

Recommended Reading

These are some of the many good resources available:

The American Diabetes Association and The American Dietetic Association Family Cookbook (Volumes I and II). Englewood Cliffs, NJ: Prentice-Hall, Inc., 1980 and 1984.

The American Heart Association Cookbook (Fourth Edition). New York: David McKay Company, Inc., 1984.

Brody, Jane E.: *Jane Brody's Good Food Book*, New York: W.W. Norton & Co., 1985.

Brody, Jane E.: *Jane Brody's Nutrition Book*, New York: W.W. Norton & Co., 1981.

Claiborne, Craig: *Craig Claiborne's Gourmet Diet*. New York: The New York Times Book Co., Inc., 1980.

Farquhar, John: *The American Way of Life Need Not Be Hazardous to Your Health*, New York: W.W. Norton & Company, 1979.

Food and Nutrition Board: *Recommended Dietary Allowances*. (Ninth Edition). Washington DC: National Academy of Sciences, 1980.

Gardner, Joseph L., ed., Johanna Dwyer, Victor Herbert, and Jerome L. Knittle, (Board of Consultants): *Eat Better, Live Better*. Pleasantville, NY: Reader's Digest Association, 1982.

Gutin, Bernard with Gail Kessler: *The High-Energy Factor*. New York: Random House, 1983.

Hamilton, Eva and Eleanor Whitney: *Nutrition: Concepts and Controversies* (Third Edition). St. Paul: West Publishing Co., 1985.

Herbert, Victor and Stephen Barrett: *Vitamins and "Health" Foods: The Great American Hustle*. Philadelphia: George F. Stickley Co., 1981.

Kraus, Barbara: *The Barbara Kraus 1986 Revised Edition Calorie Guide to Brand Names & Basic Foods*. New York: New American Library (Signet), 1986.

Lappé, Frances Moore: *Diet for a Small Planet*. New York: Ballantine Books, 1982.

Mirkin, Gabe: *Getting Thin*. Boston: Little, Brown and Co., 1983.

Robertson, Laurel, Carol Flinders, and Bronwen Godfrey: *Laurel's Kitchen: A Handbook for Vegetarian Cookery and Nutrition*. New York: Bantam Books, Inc., 1982.

Stare, Fredrick and Virginia Aronson: *Your Basic Guide to Nutrition*. Philadelphia: George F. Stickley Co., 1983.

U.S. Department of Agriculture: *Food 2*. Chicago: The American Dietetic Association, 1982.

U.S. Department of Agriculture: *Food 3*. Chicago: The American Dietetic Association, 1982.

U.S. Department of Agriculture: *Nutritive Value of Foods*. Washington, DC: Superintendent of Documents, U.S. Government Printing Office, 1985.

U.S. Department of Agriculture and the U.S. Department of Health and Human Services: *Nutrition and Your Health: Dietary Guidelines for Americans* (Second Edition). Washington, DC: Superintendent of Documents, U.S. Government Printing Office, 1985. (Single copies available without charge from the Consumer Information Center, Dietary Guidelines, Pueblo, CO 81009).

White, Alice and the Society for Nutrition Education: *The Family Health Cookbook*. New York: David McKay Company, Inc., 1980.

For further information on improving nutrition, you may write to:

American Dental Association
Bureau of Health Education
  and Audiovisual Services
211 East Chicago Avenue
Chicago, IL 60611

American Diabetes Association
National Service Center
1660 Duke Street
Alexandria, VA

American Heart Association
7320 Greenville Avenue
Dallas, TX 75231

American Society for Clinical Nutrition
9650 Rockville Pike
Bethesda, MD 20814

Community Nutrition Institute
2001 S Street, N.W.
Washington, DC 20009

FDA/Office of Consumer Affairs
(HFE-88)
5600 Fishers Lane
Rockville, MD 20857

International Life Sciences
Institute—Nutrition Foundation (ILSI-NF)
1126 Sixteenth St., N.W., Suite 111
Washington, DC 20036

National Academy of Sciences
National Research Council
Food and Nutrition Board
2101 Constitution Avenue, N.W.
Washington, DC 20418

National Dairy Council
6300 N. River Road
Rosemont, IL 60018

National Clearinghouse
  for Alcohol Information
P.O. Box 2345
Rockville, MD 20852

Society for Nutrition Education
1736 Franklin Street, 9th Floor
Oakland, CA 94612

The American Medical Association
Department of Foods and Nutrition
535 North Dearborn Street
Chicago, IL 60610

The American Dietetic Association
430 North Michigan Avenue
Chicago, IL 60611

United Fresh Fruit & Vegetable
  Association
727 North Washington St.
Alexandria, VA 22314

U.S. Department of Agriculture:
Extension Service
Home Economics and Human Nutrition
Washington, DC 20250
Human Nutrition Information Service
6505 Belcrest Road
Room 325A
Federal Building
Hyattsville, MD 20782

U.S. Department of Health
and Human Services:
National Institutes of Health
Nutrition Coordinating Committee
Building 31/4B-59
9000 Rockville Pike
Bethesda, MD 20892

Recipe Index

C

Fruit-Filled "Cream" Puff Ring,   177
Fruit-Glazed Pork Kabobs,   128

G

Garden Curry,   159
Ginger Pork,   127
Graham cracker crust,   176
Grapes, green,   176, 177
Greek Bread-Box Sandwich,   171
Green beans,   144
Green Goddess Salad Dressing,   103
Gruyere Cheese,   90

H

Halibut with Mushrooms in Creamy White Wine Sauce,
   123
Hamburgers, broiled, stuffed,   115
Herb-Seasoned Potatoes,   164
Honey-Mustard Scallop Kabobs,   121
Hot Mulled Wine,   190

K

Kabobs:
   fruit-glazed pork,   128
   honey-mustard scallop,   121

L

Lasagna:
   spinach-stuffed rolls,   145
   Verde,   142
Layered Beef and Eggplant Casserole,   113
Lemon:
   Bavarian crème,   178
   minted orange ice,   179
   wine sauce,   133
Lemon-Garlic Brussels Sprouts and Carrots,   164
Lentil and Vegetable Medley,   149
Lima Bean Casserole,   151
Lime vinaigrette,   125
Linguine with Clam Sauce,   141
London Broil Pomadora,   116
Long Johns, cracked wheat,   170

M

Macaroni and cheese, old fashioned,   147
Marinated Mushrooms,   91
Mexican Dip,   89

Milk shake(s):
  cappuccino, 189
  coco-banana, 191
Minestrone, 96
Minted Orange Lemon Ice, 179
Mocha-Filled "Cream" Puffs, 181
Monterey Jack cheese, 88, 154
Mozzarella cheese, part-skim, 107, 111, 113, 115, 142,
  148, 151, 155
Muffins, banana nut, 168
Mushrooms, 123, 139, 142, 146, 152, 155, 161
  barley soup, 98
  marinated, 91
Mustard Sauce, 136

N
Nachos, 88
New England Chowder with Scallops, 99
Nouvelle Beef Stroganoff, 114
Nouvelle French Toast, 166

O
Oatmeal Scones, 173
Oats, 170, 173
Old Fashioned Macaroni and Cheese, 147
Orange(s), 138, 190
  cran-orange glazed cornish hens, 139
  cranberry walnut mold, 107
  ginger sauce for chicken, 134
  lemon ice, minted, 179
  pudding, baked, 174
  salad with spinach, 104
Oven-Fried Tomato Slices, 162

P
Parfait, strawberry, 185
Parmesan cheese, 141, 144, 145, 162
  noodle ring, 146
Pasta Fagioli, 143
Pasta Primavera, 144
Peach(es), 109, 177
  bread pudding, 184
Peanuts, 92,110,174
Peanut Butter Raisin Cookies, 180
Pear(s), 111
  poached, spiced, 183
Peas, 144

Pepper:
  green,   93, 118, 121, 126, 151, 152, 153, 155, 160, 162,
        169, 171
  red,   93, 115, 118, 130, 152, 159, 162
Pesto Sauce,   141
Phyllo bundles, with chicken and spinach,   137
Pickled Zucchini,   93
Pie:
  blueberry cream,   175
  pineapple meringue,   182
Pineapple,
  meringue pie,   182
  Slush,   189
Pita pockets,   91
  vegetable-stuffed,   169
Polynesian chicken, stir-fried,   138
Polynesian Shrimp,   122
Popovers, spiced,   166
Poppy Seed Dressing,   111
Pork:
  fruit-glazed kabobs,   128
  ginger,   127
  roast with piquant sauce,   129
  szechuan with vegetables,   130
Potato(es):
  and beef casserole,   117
  herb-seasoned,   164
  wedges with cheddar chili sauce,   92
  yogurt-topped,   163
Pudding:
  baked orange,   174
  peach bread,   184
Punch, cranorange, spiced,   188

R
Raisin(s),   92, 104, 106, 155, 156, 173, 180
  bran quick bread,   167
Ratatouille-Stuffed Peppers,   160
Red Snapper in Lime Vinaigrette,   125
Relish, corn and pepper,   93
Ribollito Soup,   101
Rice:
  brown,   155, 158
  Con Queso,   154
  crust pizza,   155
  Pilaf,   162
  white,   110, 185
Ricotta cheese, part-skim,   90, 142, 145, 154, 175, 178

S

Swiss cheese, 119
Szechuan Pork and Vegetables, 130

T
Tabouli, 106
Taco Salad, 108
Tangeloslaw, 106
Tarragon Vinegar, 103
Tomato(es), 144, 148, 150, 158, 160, 169
   mozzarella salad, 107
   oven-fried, 162
   stewed, 149
Tortillas, 88, 108
Tuna fish, canned, 147, 171
Turkey Curry, 139
turnips, 132

V
Vegetable Bean Stew, 150
Vegetable Burgers, 152
Vegetable-Stuffed Pitas, 169

W
Waffles, strawberry with cognac, 183
Walnuts, 104, 107, 135, 141
Wine, hot mulled, 190

Y
Yogurt, 89, 97, 104, 108, 110, 111, 114, 117,
   119, 123, 136, 151, 152, 169, 171, 175, 181
   strawberry pops, 186
   -topped potatoes, 163

Z
Zucchini, 144, 159, 160
   pickled, 93